MYSTERY
OF THE BRI

The Western Isles

Glen Vaudrey

Typeset by Jonathan Downes,
Cover and Layout by MisterOrange for CFZ Communications
Using Microsoft Word 2000, Microsoft , Publisher 2000, Adobe Photoshop CS.
Edited and proofed by Jon and Dizzy Ms Lizzy

Photographs © 2009 CFZ except where noted

First published in Great Britain by CFZ Press

**CFZ Press
Myrtle Cottage
Woolsery
Bideford
North Devon
EX39 5QR**

© CFZ MMIX

ISBN: 978-1-905723-30-0

Dedicated to my beautiful wife Kerry

And in memory of Dave Burke, a gentlemen and a scholar truly missed

CONTENTS

Acknowledgments

I would like to thank the following for their help and assistance: Geoff Mahoney, for all things faery re-lated; Carl Horrocks, for supplying all you need to know about rocks; Dr Nicholas and Kathleen Gane, the finest landlords you could wish for; and Patricia Macleod for help with the Gaelic. Thanks to Callum Wallace and David Maclennan for providing helpful information and to Elizabeth Robson for her help and advice. Also my family for their encouragement, and all the good folk at the CFZ, for the opportunity to write this book.

The Mystery Animals of the British Isles

More years ago than I care to remember, my first wife bought me a birthday present. It was a book about the mystery animals of Britain and Ireland, and I devoured it avidly. When I finished I was horribly disappointed: it had covered the mystery cats of the country in some depth, as it had done with the black dog legends, with a smattering of more arcane 'things' (as the late, great Ivan T. Sanderson would doubtless have dubbed them) such as the Owlman of Mawnan, and the Big Grey Man of Ben McDhui. But there was *so* much that I knew that the author had simply left out.

Where were the mystery pine martens of the westcountry? Where were the Sutherland polecats? Where was the mysterious butterfly known as Albin's Hampstead eye? This was an Australian butterfly, the type specimen of which was caught in a cellar in Hampstead (hence the name) but no-one knows how or why. Where were the butterflies, moths, birds and even mammals known from the British Isles on the basis of a handful of specimens only? And where were the local oddities; the semi-folkloric beasts only known from a specific location?

Although at the time I had no pretensions to being a writer, I started to collect information from around the country, and with the benefit of hindsight it is probably with my disappointment with my 27th birthday present that the seeds of what would eventually grow into the Centre for Fortean Zoology were planted.

Nearly twenty years later to the day, I was sitting in my garden at the Centre for Fortean Zoology [CFZ] in North Devon, sharing a bottle of wine with my wife, Corinna and my old friends, Richard Freeman and Mike Hallowell. The subject of my disappointing 27th birthday present came up, and someone suggested that we do our best to redress the balance. CFZ Press, the publishing arm of the CFZ, has become the largest dedicated Fortean zoological publishers in the world, and we are now in the position to put my vague day-dreams of a couple of decades ago into action.

We decided that rather than trying to publish one enormous tome covering the mystery animals of the whole of the British Isles (which - by the way - geographically, if not politically, includes the Republic of Ireland, but excludes the Channel Islands) we would be much happier presenting this vast array of data in a series of books, each covering a county or two. Then we realised the enormity of what we were proposing: the series would probably end up being something in the region of forty volumes in length!

However, never folk to back away from a challenge, we decided to go ahead with the project, and now the first books in the series are being published.

We argued the toss for months over how we were going to format the series. For a long time we were intending to have a rigid format for all the books, somewhat akin to the Observer's books of the British countryside. But then we decided 'No'. There are as many kinds of researcher as there are mystery animal, and it would - we felt - be more in keeping with the ethos of the CFZ, if we allowed each researcher to present his or her findings in their own inimitable style. The books, therefore, will reflect the character of the individual author.

Some will be poetic verging on mystical. Some will be matter-of-fact scientific. Some will be from the point of view of a naturalist, and some from the point of view of a folklorist. Some will be short; some will be long. Some will be full of scientific theorising, and some full of metaphysical speculation. But one thing is sure: whoever gets one of these volumes for their 27th birthday present...

...They won't be disappointed!

Some of the books in the series are by long-established writers within the field of Fortean publishing.

Others, like this one, are written by relative newcomers. Glen wrote to me one day and offered to write this book for us. I asked him for a synopsis and a sample chapter, and was blown away by his sheer depth of knowledge, and his humble and self-effacing use of the English language.

He soon became a regular on the CFZ Bloggo, and the rest - as they say - is history.

Jonathan Downes
Director, Centre for Fortean Zoology
Woolfardisworthy,
North Devon,
June 25th 2009

Introduction

My aim with this book is to introduce you to the many wonderful mystery animals that have put in an appearance in the Western Isles over the years; from the darkest days of the Middle Ages, right up to the modern day. From the far north and the rocky slopes of Sule Sgeir, to the golden beaches of Islay, unusual creatures are to be found. On dark and lonely nights faery dogs travel the highways and byways, while on deserted beaches mermaids sit and comb their hair.

But don't be fooled into thinking that these creatures are restricted to folklore. There are plenty of well-known animals to be found here, even if they are well and truly lost. Animals such as Albert the lonely albatross, who forlornly searches the northern skies for a mate, seemingly unaware that he is around five thousand miles adrift from the rest of his clan. And while the hills of Mull are the *last* place that you would expect to find a big cat stalking its prey, reports have been coming in for over twenty years of just such an animal having been sighted.

For those unfamiliar with the Western Isles, the term is used to describe a couple of island chains to be found off the north west coast of Scotland. The most remote islands are the Outer Hebrides, which lie in the Atlantic Ocean between 30 and 60 miles from the Scottish mainland; an archipelago consisting of around 200 islands, islets, and skerries forming an arc 130 miles long from north to south. Despite the large number of islands in the chain, only around twenty have a surface area of more than three square miles, and only fourteen of the isles are now inhabited. The total landmass consists of around 1,158 square miles, with a quarter of this area consisting of lochs and lochans, which contain around a sixth of Britain's freshwater. With a population that hovers around the 28,000 mark, it leaves a lot of empty space for mystery animals to go largely unnoticed.

The Inner Hebrides (as the name suggests) can be found nearer to the Scottish mainland, with the most northerly and largest isle in the chain - Skye - being so close as to be connected to the mainland by a bridge. The chain consists of around a further thirteen islands that stretch to the south. The most southerly island in the group - Islay - lies as close to the coast of Antrim in Northern Ireland, as it does to the Scottish mainland.

The aim of this book is to draw together for the first time reports and tales of the creatures seen on land, on inland waters, and in the surrounding seas, to give the definitive guide to the mystery animals of the Western Isles.

I hope you have as much fun reading this book as I had writing it.

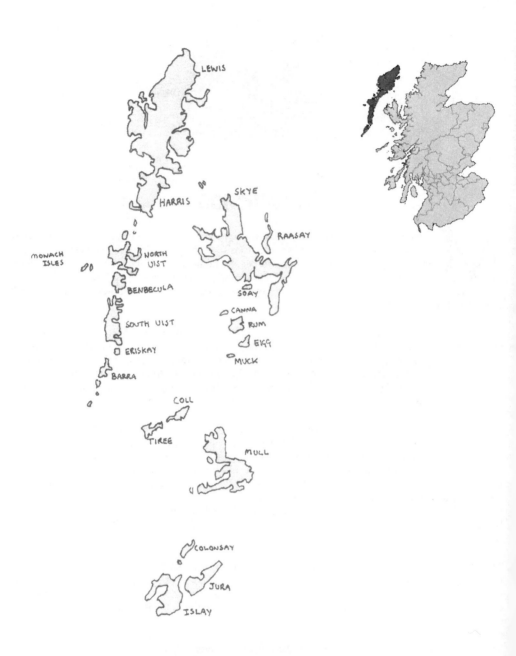

The Western Isles

BIRDS

The Great Auk/Garefowl (*Alca impennis*)

On 3rd June 1844, three men clambered across the Icelandic island of Eldey chasing the last wild great auks. On the island they find two birds, and give chase in what will turn out to be a one-sided race: the two great auks, with their little legs, and stump-like wings, waddle away as fast as they can, but there is no way that they can reach the sea. And as a result, the last two birds are caught and have their necks broken for their troubles. And that, so history would have it, is the end of the great auk! So what are we to make of the report of the bird found swimming off the isle of Skye some 36 years later?

The great auk is another one of those lost birds, ranking alongside the dodo for its unfortunate demise at the hands of man. A striking bird, it stood 75cm (30 inches) with bold black and white colouring, eyes

described as being hazel in colour, and with a distinctive outsized beak. While it was related to the razorbill (*Alca torda*) it would appear to more closely resemble the penguin. Its wings were tiny in proportion to the size of the body, but they remained wing-shaped, unlike the penguins with their more flipper-like appendages. However, but like the penguins' wings, they were incapable of flight, while being ideally suited to propelling the bird through the water. This is understandable as the great auk *did* spend the greater part of its year at sea. It is recorded by Martin Martin (so good they named him twice) in his book *A late voyage to St Kilda*, published way back in 1698, that the great auks arrived on that island in mid May each year, and would remain there until late June, when once more they would be off out to sea. The cost, of course, of this adaptation to life at sea, was that its mobility on land would be restricted. If only they could have run, they might have given those Icelanders the slip. Ultimately, their misfortune was that they came to be restricted to only a small number of nesting sites, that once known, provided easy pickings to passing sailors who fancied an auk-shaped snack.

At one time, the nesting range of these birds stretched from northern Canada to Iceland, and all

RAIDERS OF THE LOST AUK: Nowadays, all that is left of this remarkable bird is paintings, engravings, and a few forlorn museum specimens (Belgium, top left; Leipzig, top right, London, facing.)

the way down to St Kilda, an island better known today for the evacuation of its population in the 1930s. The occasional bird would be sighted in the area, and such was the case in 1821, when two men and two boys spotted one as they sailed around a low sea-facing cliff and decided that they would catch it. The boat travelled further around the island. The plan was to drop the two men off. They were then to make their way towards the Great Auk from the rear, cutting off any escape route back across the land. As the two men crept across, the two boys rowed the boat back to where they had first sighted the bird, and waited.

No matter how stealthily the men crept across the ground, they still made enough noise for the keen hearing of the great auk to pick out their presence. As if knowing what was in store for it, the bird decided it was time to head for the sea and safety. It jumped off the low cliff, and unfortunately straight into the arms of one of the boys in the boat, who had been waiting to cut off its escape.

Despite being caught in such a cunning trap, luck was still on the side of the bird, as it was decided to keep it alive, and eventually it was presented to a Mr. Stevenson - the engineer for the Board of the Commissioners of the Northern Lighthouses - who, along with the Reverend John Fleming, intended to keep the bird until its eventual death; and then pass it to the University Museum at Edinburgh. The Reverend Fleming went on to publish a description of the bird in *The Edinburgh Philosophical Journal* for 1824.

'The bird was emaciated, and had the appearance of being sickly, but in the course of a few days became sprightly, having been plentifully supplied with fresh fish, and permitted occasionally to sport in the water with a cord fastened to one of its legs to prevent escape. Even in this state of restraint it performed the motion of diving and swimming under the water with rapidity that set all pursuit from a boat defiance. A few white feathers were at this time making their appearance on

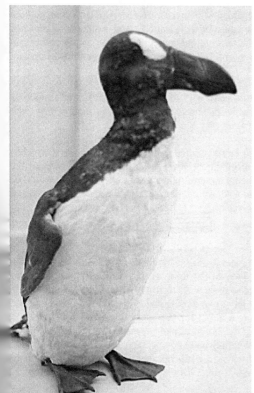

the sides of its neck and throat, which increased considerably during the following week, and left no doubt that like its congeners, the blackness of the throat feathers of summer is exchanged for white during the winter season.'

It would be during another one of those restrained swims near the entrance to the Firth of Clyde, that the plucky fellow would somehow manage to slip his tether, and make good his escape to the open seas once more.

The next great auk captured on St Kilda would not be so lucky. This sorry tale takes place around 20 years later, during the month of July. It occurred on the island of Stac-an-Armin - one of the St Kilda group of islands. If the previous great auk had been a rare sighting in the isles, by the 1840s the bird's existence would have been almost mythical.

Stac-an-Armin is a bleak rock stack jutting boldly out of the Atlantic Ocean, just off the coast of the Island of Boreray. On that fateful July day, five men travelled in their rowing boat out from the main island of St Kilda (Hirta) out hunting for sea birds. They landed safely upon the island, and while wandering around the rock, they spied a lone great auk asleep on a ledge. One of the group - Malcolm MacDonald - raced across to the sleeping bird, and firmly grabbed hold of its neck. Understandably, the bird

was less than impressed, and struggled to escape, but to no avail. There was no escape from Malcolm's grasp. It wasn't long before the others arrived at the scene, and tied its legs together. Once securely bound, the bird was carried back down the slope to their bothy.

Already things were looking pretty bleak for the bird, and it wasn't going to get any better. Soon after the capture the weather took a turn for the worse, and a storm started to pick up. So bad was it that the five men were confined to their little bothy for three days. To add to their hardship, their captive great auk started to make a great noise, calling out loudly. And whenever anyone went near the bird, it would open its mouth, and lash about with its beak; on one occasion, coming close to cutting the rope confining it, with its razor-like bill. As the storm intensified, and the auk's calls grew louder, an idea started to form in the men's minds that this abnormally large bird of a type that they had never seen before, was - of course - not a bird at all, but a witch. For three days, they were holed up in the wind-blasted shelter, before one of the men - Lauchlán McKinnon - finally snapped; frightened out of his mind, and convinced that the great auk was the cause of their trouble. You would think that just letting the bird go would have been enough to ease the tension, but something as soft as that wasn't on Lauchlán's mind! After all, they weren't dealing with a bird, but a witch. Lauchlán urged his fellows on to kill the beast, and so they did.

It took an hour for them to beat the unfortunate bird to death with of two large stones, and as soon as they were sure of its demise, they threw its pulped body out into the storm, for it to land behind their bothy.

Such was the sorry fate of one of the last great auks to be seen in the British Isles. Or *maybe* it was just the end of a shape-changing storm-causing witch. Unfortunately, there is no indication of whether the storm ceased after the bird's death, so I will go for it being an unfortunate great auk after all. It would be only another four years before the last two *known* great auks were killed, making the species extinct; and only another ninety years before the St Kildans themselves became extinct. Funny old world.

But the story doesn't end there.

It was around 1850, when two men - a Mr. Mackenzie and Malcolm Macleod - were walking along the shore on the coast of Skye. As seemed to be the fashion of the time, as they walked along, Macleod would have a go at blasting apart any bird he happened to pass, with his trusty rifle. As they continued to stroll along, they chanced to see a bird that - based solely upon its size and shape - they at first guessed as being a great northern diver. This was too tempting a target for the gun-toting Macleod, who soon brought his sights to bear upon the hapless bird, promptly shot at it, and successfully killed the unfortunate creature. So far out from the shore was the bird, that they had to get a boat to row out to the floating corpse. It was only upon reaching it, that they noticed the corpse was not that of the great northern diver they were expecting to find. In fact it turned out to be a bird of a type that neither man had seen before.

Collecting the body, they headed back for shore. The following day, Malcolm Macleod was once again walking along the shore, when he spied another of these odd birds. Once again, he steadied his trusty rifle, and blasted the poor creature into the next world. Once again, he retrieved the corpse, and headed back home - no doubt to the relief of any bird left bobbing upon the waters. Macleod kept the head of one of these birds as a trophy. He would later comment that before those two days, he had never seen one of these birds before, and that he never saw any of that kind again. Then, if I was one of these mystery birds, I wouldn't have gone within rifle range of him.

For thirty-five years, those two unfortunate birds would remain a mystery. But in 1880, Mr. Mackenzie revealed in conversation with R. Scott Skirving, that he believed that the bird that he had seen Malcolm Macleod shoot, was in fact a great auk. If this was indeed the case, it would have been a sighting after the supposed extinction of the bird. Certainly Skirving found the information given to him interesting enough to track down the trigger-happy Malcolm Macleod, who was in due course able to confirm the story, and to give details of the second unlucky bird. Unfortunately, the last remains of those two birds had long since been thrown away; hardly surprising, given that thirty-five years had passed since then. If they were indeed great auks, they were likely to have been the last to visit Scotland's coast.

Is it possible that the great auk still survives today? Well, at *best* it would be highly unlikely, but stranger things have been known to happen at sea! And who knows, one day one of those great northern divers that happily swim around Stornoway harbour, might turn out to be something entirely more great auk-like.

A Lonely Albatross

Many mysterious things have been seen in the air in the Western Isles. If you had happened to be on Benbecula in years gone by you, may have been nervously peering out of your window at night, watching the *Sluagh* as they raced across overhead on their way to the land of the ever-young. If you're really lucky, you might happen to see the Aurora Borealis as it plays overhead in the winter months. I can't say that I have managed to see them yet. But who knows? One day I might.

It is claimed that in the mid 1990s that most secret of US spy planes - the Aurora - was believed to have flown over Ness, leaving its unique donut-shaped exhaust trail across the sky. I wouldn't believe *that* one if I were you. But that's not to say that there aren't plenty of military aircraft flying over the isle of Lewis during the year, peaking at the times of the biannual large naval exercises. Usually I miss them, but I did manage to spot a Russian spy plane trying to sneak by while I was hanging out the washing. But all this is leading us astray, and away from the real airborne subject of this chapter, because there is - in fact - something very unusual to be seen in the skies: a bird with a giant wing span of over eight feet. But this is no North American Thunderbird cruising overhead, searching for its prey. It's just one very lost albatross, and he goes by the unimaginative name of Albert.

For the last forty years, there has been an avian stranger flying over the north Atlantic, and whether he considers himself to *really* be called Albert or not, he most certainly *is* a black-browed albatross, and he is most definitely lost. And we are not talking just in the wrong town. Nor even the wrong country. In fact not even 'just the wrong continent' is near enough to describe how off-the-albatross-beaten-track Albert is. He is actually in the wrong hemisphere, and short of being on the wrong planet, that is about as lost as it gets. If we talking distance, he is 8,000 miles from where he should be.

It seems likely that our lost albatross first appeared in the north in the late 1960s. Perhaps he was attracted by the swinging sixties, we shall never know for certain, but a black-browed albatross was first spotted on Bass Rock in the Firth of Forth on 18 May 1967. And he would reappear during the following two years. Being an eager fellow, Albert wasn't put off by being lost, and he soon started to perform his courtship ritual to no doubt bemused local seagulls and gannets. Eventually the plucky fellow must have realized that he was wasting his time on Bass Rock, and headed north in search of a mate. His travels took him all the way up to one of the most northerly places in the British Isles - the Shetland island of Unst; turning up there in 1972, when his eye was taken by the gannet colony at Hermaness. Those lady gannets must have really appealed to the hapless Albert, because despite putting his best efforts into his mating rituals, and not getting any bites, he still returned every year for the next 23 years. You would have thought that he would have got the hint by now.

When he's not bothering the ladies, Albert disappears out to sea. Where he gets to is a mystery, but he probably spends the winter months roaming over the north Atlantic, feeding on the fish he catches, and resting upon the water when not flying. It was 1995 when he was last seen at the gannet colony at Hermaness, and then he seemed to vanish for good. While he might not have been putting in an appearance at any of the known bird colonies, there were still sightings of a black-browed albatross around the coast, not only of Scotland, but of England, Wales, Ireland, and even as far south as the Channel Isles. While the sightings cover a wide geographical area, there were never any simultaneous sightings, so it would seem to be the lovelorn Albert, carrying out his long search, (though it would be nice to think it was a lonely lady black-browed albatross also out looking for love).

If, of course, it *is* Albert being sighted in these different locations, he could be searching for a very long time. It's estimated that the bird is around 47 years of age, and it would be expected that he should easily live to a ripe old age of 70, because that is the average natural age that a black-browed albatross would attain, if they get the chance, which they often don't do.

You see, in the southern hemisphere, there is a lot of long-line fishing going on, with boats trawling lines of up to 80 miles in their wake. This is having a devastating impact on the albatross population, with around 100,000 of them being snagged on the lines, resulting in their being drowned. The result of this type of fishing is that 19 of the 21 species of albatross - including the black-browed albatross - now face extinction. Perhaps Albert is aware of this carnage, and has decide that a life of abstinence is better than a short life ended by being dragged by a trawler. If only more albatrosses managed to make it north of the equator, things might not be so bad for them.

Anyway, back to Albert's reappearance in the Western Isles. In 2005, he was first noticed at the gannet colony on

EDITOR'S NOTE: Although the black-browed albatross is basically a circumpolar, southern hemisphere species, there are other records of seriously out-of-place specimens. According to Wikipedia: "A similar incident took place in the gannet colony in the Faroe Islands island of Mykines, where a Black-browed Albatross lived among the gannets for over 30 years. This incident is the reason why an albatross is referred to as a 'Gannet King' (Faroese: súlukongur) in Faroese", and G.A.C Herklots, in *Hong Kong Birds* (1968) notes an albatross of unknown species seen at Castle Peak, in the then-British Crown Colony, in 1960.

the remote rocky islet of Sula Sgeir, 40 miles north of the Butt of Lewis. So remote a place is this location, that it's possible he may have been turning up there unnoticed since his sudden disappearance from Hermaness some 10 years before.

As well as being the present abode of Albert the black-browed albatross, there is something else that happens on Sula Sgeir that attention should be drawn to. That is the annual hunt of the guga. If you have never heard the term before, a 'guga' is the name for a young gannet not yet able to fly, and it is this protected bird that the men of Ness (for some reason) seem to think is worth hunting.

Every year, around ten men set off in a fishing boat from the township of Ness on the isle of Lewis, and head for the small island of Sula Sgeir to hunt the far from fearsome guga. On arrival at the island they clamber ashore, and set up camp inside one of the deserted beehive buildings that are to be found there, between the 8,000 pairs of gannets and the hundreds of years of bird shit. The hunt itself is quite simple: the men go out in pairs amongst the chicks, and collect the unfortunate birds using a noose on the end of a pole; each bird is then passed back to the second man who administers the *coup de grâce* with a stick.

In many ways, this hunting of the birds for food mirrors what was happening on St Kilda two hundred years before, when one of those hunting trips had a great auk charged as a witch, and beaten to death. (Let's hope no one thinks that Albert the albatross is responsible for any storm, or he might well get a smack on the head). Whereas the men of St Kilda were hunting the fowl for their survival (it was said that on St Kilda the diet largely consisted of seabird, seabird eggs, and seabird chicks; either smoked or wind-dried), it has to be stated that it certainly isn't the case in Ness these days. After all, there are both a Tesco and a Co-op superstore on the island; albeit they don't sell guga, but they stock everything else you could possibly want to eat. There are probably a couple of reasons why they don't stock guga - one is that it's a rare and protected bird, and the second more important reason has to be the taste! **

While the people of Ness might think that it is well worth travelling across 40 miles of ocean to a small mucky island, and spending two weeks on it hunting the guga, not many other people find the taste worth the effort. Those who like it might describe it as being like a salty goose full of fat, while those who are in the not-eating-it camp would possibly liken it to a piece of leather with the taste of fishy beast, and if *that* doesn't tempt the taste buds, how about a duck stewed in cod liver oil? Whatever the taste, it's the foul smell that seems to be the main off-putting thing.

Of course, the reason given for the continued hunt is tradition, carrying on something that has been going on for centuries, but tradition is not necessarily *always* a good thing. If we go back once more to the example of St Kilda, we learn that the people there had a tradition whereby midwives would smear a poultice of fulmar oil and dung on the navel of a new-born child, because this had always been done. As the result of following this tradition, eight out of ten babies died of tetanus within eight days of birth; you'll

---

** EDITOR'S NOTE: One of the earliest accounts written about the Western Isles was by Dean Munro, who visited the islands in 1549. His description of Sula Sgeir (Munro, D. (1818) *Description of the Western Isles of Scotland called Hybrides, by Mr. Donald Munro, High Dean of the Isles, who travelled through most of them in the year 1594.* Miscellanea Scotica, 2.) mentions that the men of Ness sailed in their small craft to *"fetche hame thair boatful of dry wild fowls with wild fowl fedderi"*. How long before 1549 the Nessmen sailed to Sula Sgeir each year to collect the young gannets for food and feathers is not known, but it may be assumed that it was a tradition for centuries. That tradition is still carried on today. A report written in 1797 says:

> *"There is in Ness a most venturous set of people who for a few years back, at the hazard of their lives, went there in an open six-oared boat without even the aid of a compass."*

Excellent seamanship was certainly essential for the success of these expeditions - rowing across miles of turbulent Atlantic was no pleasure cruise.

The annual cull of birds has been the focus of attention of bird protectionists, who recently have tried to ban the cull completely. But tradition dies hard and the Sula Sgeir trip still goes on, with a special dispensation written into the 1954 Wild Birds Protection Act by a Statutory Order, which allows the Nessmen to continue their taste both for adventure and for the guga.

not see that practice carried on today in the hospital. Perhaps it's better to let some traditions die out.

The Black Eagle

As we have seen, late in the seventeenth century, a certain Martin Martin wrote what could be classed as a very early travel guide to the Western Isles. It gave many a handy hint, as well as a brief guide to some of the animals that you might happen to come across in the area. These animals ranged in size from the great huge man-eating whales that made the most of the floating snack known commonly as 'fishermen in a boat', to the rather small (yet certainly creepy) worm that infected a number of people in a horrific manner, (the description of which is not for the squeamish). But between those two extremes of size, there were a number of winged wonders at which to marvel, and unlike many of Martin's animals one at least showed no interest in hunting or infecting people. No, these birds were only interested in hunting deer.

You would think that an eagle that specialised in hunting deer would be a big beast, (although maybe not as big as Sinbad's Roc, would hunt elephants and carry them aloft in their mighty talons, before dropping them to earth to kill them). The black eagle of Skye wasn't such a mightily pinioned bird. In fact, it wasn't even judged to be the biggest type of eagle to live on the island at the time, being easily smaller than both the white-tailed sea eagle, *and* the golden eagle. But whatever the black eagle lacked in size, it made up for in cunning, because it had a rather unique way of hunting its prey.

So how did this small eagle hunt such large game? You may well ask. Well, what the black eagle would do, was simply to select its prey then land upon it with its talons fixed between the deer's antlers. Once securely in place, it would beat its wings around the deer's eyes, causing the creature to become distressed, and to eventually panic it into trying to run away from its tormentor. But no matter how fast the deer ran, or how violently it bucked, it couldn't shake off the black eagle from its perch between the antlers. Eventually the blinded and distressed deer would run into trouble - literally as it turned out - as it would fall into a ditch, or tumble off some precipice. Whichever trip hazard it was, the result would be the same. The deer was either crippled - or killed - in the ensuing collision with whatever solid surface into which it came into contact. Flying clear from the chaos at the very last second, the black eagle would calmly circle around, and come back for the still-warm carcass and a fresh meal of venison.

The black eagle wasn't the only eagle that caused the deaths of deer in such a manner. Another type is said to have hunted together in a group; they would fly alongside a deer, and again attempt to distract and confuse it into panicked flight, which usually ended with the deer running into something solid and terminal, or falling down a hole with equally fatal results. Once again, the final outcome would see the eagles circle back for a feast.

FAERY DOGS

The hunting dogs of the *Sluagh*

For a start the *Sluagh* isn't a creature, no matter how much it might sound like a slow-moving animal of the Amazonian rain forest, nor is it a town to be found just north of Windsor. This *Sluagh* is to do with the fairies, and believe me, it's *not* for the fairies.

Nearly every part of the country has its own wild hunt; be it Wild Edric and his hounds racing along the Welsh marches, Herne the Hunter and his baying headless hounds in Windsor Great Park, or the whist hounds of Dartmoor still chasing the spectre of Jan Trageagal on stormy nights, while in Newcastle the Gabriel hounds can still be heard on occasion. Wherever these hounds are said to visit, the aerial ghostly hunting parties are seen as harbingers of doom and death. But in the Western Isles, it wasn't the hounds of the hunt that you had to worry about; it was their owners - the members of the *Sluagh*.

'*Sluagh*' translates as 'host' or 'army', and they certainly seem to be a mixture of the two. To some, they are the spirits of mortals doomed to fly around in the ether, unable to enter into heaven until they have made good the sins that they committed in their lifetimes. The trouble with *that* type of spirit, is that they don't seem to be making any progress on the road to redemption; rather, they seem to have strayed a long way from it. They are said to live high in the clouds, and only come to earth to visit the scenes of their transgressions, arriving like a flock of birds.

But to others, the *Sluagh* are the spirit host, and this host are the fairies of the air who ride upon it. They are not the 'soft' fairies that seem to fill too many books, nor are they the type of fairies that people would look forward to having living at the bottom of the garden. The *Sluagh* are a completely different type; the old type, the type that you wouldn't like to meet. In fact I would go as far as to say these are the type that, if wise, you would actively avoid.

Tales abound of what the *Sluagh* would get up to. They would sweep down to pluck the lucky or unlucky from the ground, and transport them through the air, seeing such wonderful sights that can only be imagined; but at *what* a cost! There is the tale of how the beautiful daughter of the King of France was collected by the host as they descended to the earth, only to be carried up with them, and taken high in the air over land and sea across many miles, until she found herself cast down upon the island of Heistamal near Creagorry on Benbecula. (Just what *is* it with things washing up on that island? Be they French prin-

cesses, mermaids, globsters or 27-metre-long mystery containers; they *all* manage to hit an island little more than five miles long). The *Sluagh* had so maltreated the princess, that when she was discovered she was found to be dying from her injuries. She had only enough time to explain who she was, where she had been, and the sights that she had seen, before finally passing away. All the way from France, to be buried on Benbecula!

Nor were all the victims of the *Sluagh* from far away. If you were unlucky enough to be caught out after dark when they flew by, they might well carry you off for the night. There was a man from Benbecula who claimed that he had been taken aloft with the *Sluagh* on several occasions. Such was the experience, that he would become fearful at night, and on no account would he leave the house after dusk. When he died, it was said that it was because of the extreme exhaustion that he suffered from travelling with the *Sluagh*.

While the human residents might be able to hide indoors during the hours of darkness, there was no respite for their animals. If the *Sluagh* liked to toy with men, they equally liked to hunt the cats, dogs, sheep, and cattle that they came across on their travels. They would kill these animals with fairy darts, which they would cast from the sky with unnerving accuracy. In the morning, these flint arrowheads could be found lying alongside the dead animal. But they wouldn't always do the shooting themselves; often they would encourage - or rather *force* - their human captives to do it, and it would seem out of pure spite that they would force them to carry out the most evil of deeds. But despite their orders, there were those who would cheat them of their mischief, and aim wide. On one occasion, a man shot the cow instead of the girl milking it, fooling the *Sluagh* by producing the bloodied arrows. But if there is one impression you get about the host, it's that you wouldn't want to be around when they find out they have been cheated. I get the idea that they might well visit you in the night with something very unpleasant.

So unwelcome was a visitation by the *Sluagh,* that if there was a person dying within a household, the family would ensure that any windows and doors that faced west would be blocked, so as to deny entry to them, (it being well known that that was the direction from which they approached).

But sometimes even locking the door wouldn't work, as the following tale from Benbecula demonstrates.

There were two men sheltering inside one of the long-houses, alongside the calves that occupied one end of the primitive building. They passed their time talking beside the peat fire that burned away, illuminating the room with its light. Before you get the notion that this sounds like a pleasant life, just imagine the acrid peat smoke gathering in the roof space, and the smell that - no doubt - emitted from the cattle at the other end of the long-house. It is not for nothing that cows are held responsible for emitting enough methane to aid global warming.

Suddenly their noisome evening was interrupted as the door was flung open, introducing some fresh air into the room. But it wasn't just fresh air that burst upon the startled pair; there was also a couple of faery dogs. The dogs were chained together by a leash made of precious metal that was itself set with glistening jewels that shone brightly in the firelight, sending coloured rays around the room. Even as the pair of herders sat - stunned - no doubt, jaws dropped, looking at the mystical dogs and at the small fortune that lay about their necks, they were soon snapped back to reality (if that's what you would call this) by a mystic voice that came from beyond the door, calling the hounds.

Slender fay, slender fay!
Mountain-traveller, mountain traveller!
Black-faery, black faery!
Lucky-treasure, lucky treasure!
Grey-hound, grey-hound!
Seek-beyond, seek-beyond!

It took just a moment for the two great faery dogs to rush back out. Fascinated by what they had just witnessed, the two men followed the dogs out into the chill air. Once outside, they gazed up to the sky, and saw the *Sluagh* in all their majesty, with their hounds on their leashes, and hawks upon their wrists. The men watched the hunting party travel westward, while all around them, the heavens rang with the sounds of the *Sluagh*, their voices mingling with the sound of celestial bells as they gave orders to their hunting dogs. It took only a moment for them to head off further west, flying from Benbecula out over the sea and across the Monach Isles, out past St Kilda, and even past that far outpost of Rockall as they raced out across the heavens on their way to the land of the ever young, Tir-nan-Og.

The faery dogs of Tiree

We have already met the faery hounds of the *Sluagh* as they career across the heavens in search of their prey on Benbecula. But the hounds of the *Sluagh* are only one kind of faery dogs recorded in the Western Isles. The next ones to look at are the faery dogs once bserved on the small isle of Tiree.

Tiree is one of the Inner Hebrides, and is to be found to the west of the isle of Mull, immediately south of neighbouring Coll. With the exception of a couple of hills, one in the north and the other in the south, the land barely rises 50 feet above sea level.

It is home to the faery dog known in these parts as the *cu sith*. This mystical dog is not one to be easily mistaken for a run-of-the-mill hound. For a start, it is a big beast; its size often described as being comparable to thatr of a two-year-old heifer, certainly not easily mistaken for a West Highland terrier. As befitting an animal of this stature, its footprints are reported as being as big as the spread of an adult's hand. With its tail coiled over its back, or equally plaited, and hanging down behind again, this would give a clue to its being far from run-of-the-mill. Of course, I have so far failed to mention the biggest giveaway that suggests the animal is far from the norm, and that is the colour - it's green! Yes, green, with the shade getting lighter towards its massive paws.

As befitting an unnatural beast of this size, it likes to haunt the dark night, and - believe me - there are plenty of dark nights up here, far from all the light pollution that you get in large parts of the United Kingdom. It's worth a trip up here just to experience the dark night, with the sky full of thousands of stars. Who knows, you might even come across a *cu sith* as it silently moves along in a straight line, giving the impression that nothing could restrain it as it plods along with purpose. Of course, if you *do* happen to come across such a beast one dark and lonely night, there is something that you should bear in mind: if it starts to bark, there could be trouble. Not that it is often said to bark, but when it does, it's reputed to be very loud. Tradition has it that the *cu sith* only barks just the three times, and that on the third bark things get a bit terminal for the those hearing that fateful noise. But as luck would have it, so the story goes, the *cu sith* does take its time to get around to that third fateful bark. So if you are unlucky enough to happen across said hound, and it starts to bark, consider the first bark as the starting pistol firing, giving you plenty of time to give it legs in the opposite direction, whilst trying to find somewhere out of 'bark shot', or failing that, you could always put your faith in some good quality ear protection, and keeping your fingers crossed.

In our first encounter with the *cu sith* of Tiree, the observer decided that discretion was the better part of valour. Many years ago, so the story goes, on a chilly winter's night, an islander was travelling across the moor near Kennavarra, when he happened to observe a strange creature (with which he was unfamiliar) crouching amongst the nearby sand dunes. While he might not have known what the creature was, he certainly decided that it would be better to go home by an alternative route, and so he started off back in a different direction, perhaps noting that it is better to let sleeping dogs lie.

The next morning, feeling a bit braver, and making the most of the all-important daylight, he set off back across the moor, heading to the place where he had seen the creature. When he arrived at the dunes, he was relieved to see that the beast had gone, but it hadn't gone without leaving a trace - for there in the sand it had left mighty footprints. Bending down next to the prints, our intrepid islander was able to measure them, and discovered that they were comparable in size to the palm of his hand. Being a curious fellow, he decided to follow the footprints, so off he went for some distance before they came to an abrupt end. Putting all the clues together, the islander was sure that the animal he had seen the previous night had been the *cu sith,* for he knew from the size of the prints, and the way that they had vanished, that they didn't belong to any ordinary dog from Tiree, and considering that the island is quite small, he would have been sure to have known if any of his neighbours owned such a dog.

Of course, the dunes are not the only location on Tiree where the *cu sith* was to be found. For a start, there's the cavern known as 'the lair of the Faery Dog', which as the name suggests, *does* give an idea of what you might find there. It gained its name from being a place on the island where the barking of the faery dog could often be heard. Of course, with the reputation that the barking carried with it, you would have to wonder why anyone would go out of their way to hear it. Or then again perhaps the name was chosen to give you *plenty* of warning of what to expect.

But it was in *another* cave that a shepherd was to have a close encounter with a couple of faery dogs, or rather, faery puppies. He had been out in the wilds looking after his sheep, and - as is usual for the isles - the wind was blowing, and when that wind blows things can get very chilly. Not wishing to get cold himself, the shepherd decided to shelter behind a large rock. If he thought his blood was getting cold in the wind, that was nothing to the ice that must have flowed through his veins when he discovered that he wasn't the only one sheltering behind that rock. There, before him in a hollow hidden from view by the rock, lay two large pups. When he got up close, he realised they were a lot larger than he would have expected; they were easily larger than his own dog - a full grown collie. No doubt he was thinking that there was only one kind of dog known in the area that could have such large offspring, and without another thought, he made his retreat from the scene; all the time keeping a look out, in case the parents should come home.

But it wasn't only the sand dunes and caves of Tiree where you might expect to have the *cu sith* appear to disturb your day. There was the tale told by an old woman of the isle, who claimed that in her youth she and a neighbour had been searching the beach for driftwood; a necessity on an island with few trees. It was while searching the beach, that the pair of them heard a deep booming bark of a dog. Her companion was in no doubt that they had heard the first of the *cu sith's* three barks. Upon hearing the noise, she had grabbed her neighbour by the arm, and dragged her home; concerned that if they did not make the most of the warning, the *cu sith* would get them. Of course, we can gather that they never heard that fateful third bark.

Sometimes the *cu sith* came to visit you, rather than you crossing its path - as the final tale from Tiree demonstrates. It was in the area of the summer sheilings that border Hynish bay, that we next encounter the *cu sith*. In centuries past, during the summer, the crofters' cattle would be sent up to higher pastures in the hills. And in this *particular* case, the animals were taken up to the base of Hynish hill. As was the custom, someone would accompany the animals to their summer location, to ensure that none of them went astray. In this case, two boys had gone with the cattle to the new pasture, and were set the task of looking after them during the night. They no doubt started off with the best of intentions, but it wouldn't take long for the pair of them to decide that spending all night in the open wasn't going to be that great.

As the evening wore on, the boys started to feel tired, and no doubt they were certain that no harm would befall the cattle if they nipped off into a little shieling hut for a short nap. Just as they were on the verge of sleep, they heard the noise of something heavy walking across the turf roof of the hut. As they lay there, shivering, the noise was followed by a series of weird howlings that called out into the quiet night. Lucky for them, it wasn't barking this time. Eventually the howling stopped, and the mystery animal left the roof, and the boys eventually got some sleep. In the morning, when they awoke, they decided that it would be safe enough to look for traces of what may have been on the roof during the night - possibly to see if the events had been real, or just a dream. As it turned out, the events seemed to have been very real, for there on the turf roof, they could see the great paw prints left by the *cu sith* that had visited them the night before.

All that glistens isn't gold; mind you it used to be

It would appear that the Western Isles are fair littered with litters of faery dogs, but the sightings tend to become scarcer the further north you get. So while you might consider yourself hard pressed not to cross paths with one in the Inner Hebrides (remember to run home before the third bark) the chances of seeing one by the time you get to the Outer Hebrides start to prove harder - but not impossible, as the sighting of a faery dog in South Uist in 1948 so easily demonstrates. Perhaps the reason why sightings of faery dogs become harder the further north you get, is because of the wide open expanses where these phantom canines can happily wander about, barking to their heart's content. Or it could just be that they share the same characteristic that the faery dog of Luskentyre beach possesses; namely invisibility. You have to admit that does make sightings just that *little* bit harder.

The beach at Luskentyre is a very impressive site for the faery dog to be haunting. It consists - when the tide is out - of a beach of golden sands, that measures a full two miles long, and is up to half a mile at its widest. No doubt, it is the sheer remoteness (that's remote in the sense of being near a road, and on an island with ten flights arriving each day, and around the same number of ferries docking) of the Western

Isles beaches, that make them so uncrowded and clean. Of course, they can be like any other beach; not much fun when it's lashing it down with rain, and the wind is howling around your ears, but the weather isn't really that bad all the time.

An old story tells of how, once upon a time, the golden sands of Luskentyre beach really *were* golden - the grains on that particular beach consisting of pure gold. And being such a generous beach, it seemed not to mind if people local to the area took the odd spadeful every now and again for their own use. It must have been the only time that the local economy worked to the gold standard. Now, before you pack your spade and buy that return ticket, it's only fair to tell you that the days of free gold have long gone. You will see why, as the old tale concludes. One day, a greedy avaricious man came to the beach, and he wasn't thinking of just taking a little bit of gold to buy a loaf or a sheep, or whatever else he needed. No, he had bigger plans.

So, on the fateful day, our greedy fellow turns up on the beach, dragging his donkey along behind him. While the donkey makes the most of its feed-bag, the man gets to work with his spade, and begins to fill the panniers that are strapped across the animal's back. It's not long before the poor donkey is starting to sag under the weight. Luckily for the donkey, the greedy man decides that he has enough gold, and with a dramatic flourish, he throws away his spade, and leads the heavily laden donkey off the beach, and heads to where his boat lies, tied up at the harbour. You see, our greedy man has a cunning idea. Obviously he has had enough of the weather, and fancies a change of scenery on the mainland, where - of course - he will get more for his gold. Well, actually, he is counting on selling the gold on the mainland for double the price (a reverse principle applies on the island today, where it was noted in a recent trial that a drug dealer was charging double the mainland price; that's islands for you). It doesn't take long to load the panniers onto the boat, much to the relief of the donkey, which is then set free. After all, the greedy man will be able to buy himself a whole fleet of luxury horses, when he sells his gold. Casting off from the shore, the little boat gently makes its way out to sea - no doubt its sole occupant is making a mental note of all the things that he will be able to buy with his new-found wealth. Maybe he was even wondering why no-one else had thought of doing this kind of thing before. Well, he soon received the answer to *that* question, as all of a sudden his little boat is sucked deep under the water, dragging the man to his death, and taking the gold to the seabed. I would like to imagine that there was an evil chuckle from the sky at the same time, but whether accompanied by such laughter or not, the golden sands on the beach turned from true gold to just rather nice sand, as punishment for the greedy man's transgression.

So now that the gold has gone, that just leaves the faery dog or *cu sith* to be found on the beach, or possibly just its footprints. The traditional stories refer only to the footprints being found. These are not easily mistaken for normal dog prints - being far bigger than those that even the largest of true dogs could leave behind in the wet sand.

When Alasdair Alpin MacGregor, the author of all things Hebridean-related, was travelling around the Western Isles researching his books in the 1930s, he eventually found himself on the no-longer-golden sands at Luskentyre. Recalling the traditional tales of the sightings of the faery dog, he proceeded to try and track down a witness. As luck would have it, his path soon crossed that of a young man who was herding some cows. Being the investigative bloke that he was, Alasdair asked the young man if he had ever heard tales of the faery dog that was said to leave its prints upon the beach. Much to his surprise, the young man confirmed that not only had he *heard* of the tale of the faery dog, but that he himself had come across a set of the large canine prints on that lonely beach. He went on to tell Alasdair that while he had never seen anything other than the footprints, he *did* know of a number of people on Harris whose encounters with the animal had not just been restricted to paw prints, but who had both heard (and on some occasions actually seen) the faery dog. The young cowherd would proceed to show his companion the site where he had come across the footprints in the damp sand, and as Alasdair would record in the *The Ghost Book,*

> 'This is the bit where myself saw the Cu-Sith's footprints' he now told me and in a whisper, lest seal or seabird should overhear. We were very much alone at the time; and I could not but feel my informant was letting me into a secret not to be divulged. Perhaps, he was warning me, lest one tarried too late by this haunted shore land.'

Perhaps the young man suspected the beach itself had a sentient presence of its own, perhaps recalling the fate of the greedy man and his boat-load of gold. Or perhaps he was just recalling the threat the faery dog held. And as the old tales of this beach confirmed, it wasn't only the third bark of the *cu sith* that you had to fear - for it was also told that those who stepped into the tread of those large otherworldly paw prints, and followed their course, would be driven to madness. So if you do happen to come across a set of mysterious paw prints on the beach, think twice before stepping in them, and if you choose to do so, don't say you haven't been warned.

Black Dog of Ardura: the doggy dark omen

So far the mystery dogs of the Western Isles have been restricted to sightings of the faery hounds of the *Sluagh,* as they race across the heavens, hunting down any mortal unlucky enough to be out when they pass overhead, on their way to the land of the ever-young, Tir-nan-Og. Or to sightings of the *cu sith* - the monstrous hound that stalked across the lonely places in the Isles, whose gigantic footprints litter the deserted beaches of Harris, and whose first two barks were a warning to run, because if you heard that fateful third bark, the hound would be down on you like a dirty-great-big-dog ready for a human feast. But the third bark of the *cu sith* wasn't the only canine threat to be found in the Hebrides. The isle of Mull in the Inner Hebrides, has its own canine critter to watch out for, in the form of the Black Dog of Ardura: for to see this particular dog spelt death (maybe only for a dyslexic) for someone in the area.

There are a couple of instances of the Black Dog of Ardura making an appearance recorded in *The Ghost Book* by Alasdair Alpin MacGregor. Both the sightings come courtesy of Dr Reginald MacDonald, who had more than a couple of encounters with the animal, which could hardly have been of much comfort to any patient he was on his way to visit, as the next tale will show.

It was the year 1909, and Chief Murdoch Gillian MacLaine was a very ill, bedridden old man; a virtual prisoner in Lochbuie House. But despite his predicament, he did have the benefit of being able to call on Dr MacDonald. Whether the chief would have been so keen if he had known about the good doctor's reputation for seeing the black dog, is another matter. Dr MacDonald's first run-in with the dog, came following a visit to the chief, that resulted in him being too late to make that evening's ferry across to the metropolis that is Oban. Still, it wasn't like the doctor would have to sleep rough that night at the ferry terminal: he was able to spend the night as a guest at Lochbuie House. The next morning, having had the benefit of a good night's sleep, he was up early; so early it was still dark. His intention being to get to the ferry terminal in time to meet the steamer that would be returning to Oban that morning. On opening the front door to let himself out, he was surprised to see a black dog race past him into the house. Thinking that the poor dog must be one of the household pets that had been accidentally locked out all night, he opened the second inner door, to let the dog inside the house proper. After ensuring that the dog was

LEWIS

HARRIS SKYE

RAASAY

MONACH ISLES NORTH UIST

BENBECULA SOAY

SOUTH UIST CANNA RUM

ERISKAY EIGG MUCK

BARRA

COLL

TIREE MULL

COLONSAY

JURA

ISLAY

safely inside, he closed both sets of doors behind him, and continued on his way to the waiting trap that was to take him to the ferry at Craignure.

While making the journey to the ferry, he passed the time in conversation with his driver. Having travelled with him many times previously, most of the topics were nothing special, but things suddenly got a little more interesting when Dr MacDonald happened to mention, that on his way out, he had had to let in one of the household dogs that had been left out all night. You can imagine the doctor's surprise when the driver, in a state of shock, responded: "you let the dog in?"

Obviously, the doctor felt he was missing something. Perhaps the dog hadn't been house-trained. But the driver went on to explain *why* he was so concerned. He told his stunned passenger that this wasn't just any old dog. No, this *particular* dog was special; it was a phantom creature, a ghostly herald of bad news. While it might have looked just like a big black dog that on first glance could pass for a retriever, the animal was no mortal canid. It was known on Mull as the 'Black Dog of Ardura', and seeing it was a sure sign that someone was about to shuffle off this mortal coil, and this being the case, the future wasn't looking too bright, or - come to think of it - too long, for Chief Murdoch Gillian MacLaine.

Whether the good doctor sank back into his seat on hearing this news, is not recorded, but I am sure that he was now a little more concerned about letting the dog in. Still, he may have been looking on the bright side; at least he wouldn't be needing a return ticket.

A little while later, the news of the death of Chief Murdoch Gillian MacLaine was announced. It appeared that during the week between his death and burial, Lochbuie House suffered a haunting. Strange, terrifying noises were heard, furniture moved about, and the piano played by itself during the night, emitting a strange and eerie noise. However, after the chief's burial, the disturbances ceased. Perhaps the ghostly presence of the chief was running around the house, trying to kick a ghostly dog.

Now, you would think that the chances of seeing a ghostly dog *once* would be hard enough, but it appears that Dr Macdonald was going to have another encounter with the Black Dog of Ardura. It was five years later, when the good doctor would have his next run-in with the cryptid canine. This time he was travelling back from visiting an old man in the village of Lochbuie. Heading towards the village of Salen, he was driving up the steep Ardura hill, when he started to hear what seemed like the unnatural yowling of a dog coming from somewhere in the woods nearby. It wasn't just hearing the odd howling. As the car slowly travelled up the hill, he saw - illuminated in the beam of his headlights - the unmistakable form of the black dog emerging from the wood. It then proceeded to run ahead of him for a distance before it vanished. Having seen the dog previously, and knowing what ensued following his previous encounter, it probably didn't come as too great a surprise the next morning, when he was told that the old man he had visited was no more. After this second incident, it appears that Dr Reginald MacDonald had no more sightings of the dog. Whether this is really as a result of never seeing it again, or just the fact that he stopped reporting sightings is unclear. Certainly, if word got out that every time he saw the dog a

Loch Buie House,
Isle of Mull.
N.B.

14/11 - 15.

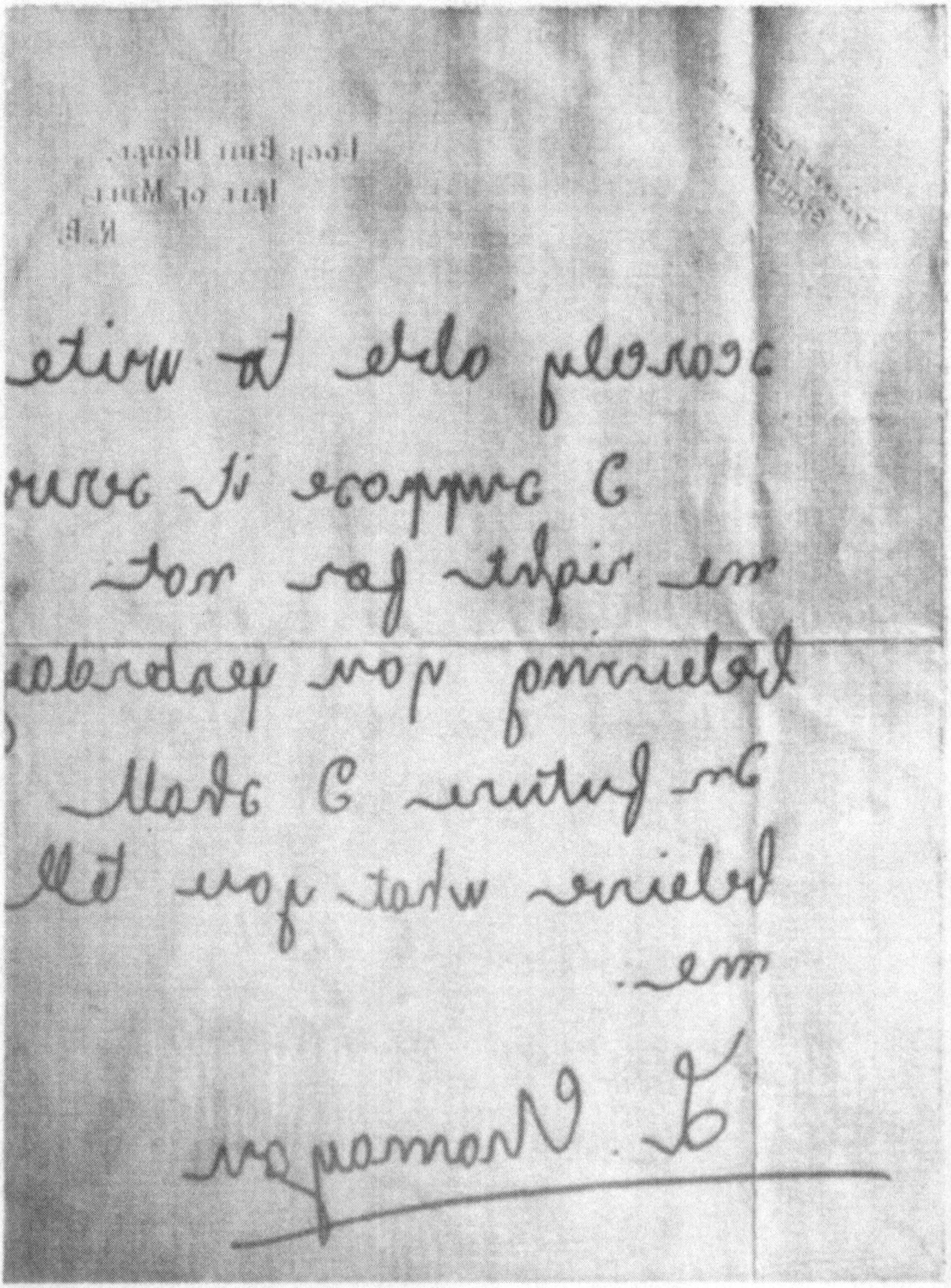

scarcely able to write

I suppose it came

me right for not

Returning you yesterday

In future I shall

desire what you tell

me.

A. Thomson

patient died, it's likely that there wouldn't be a great demand for his services.

While the doctor may not have recorded further sightings of the Black Dog of Ardura, he was connected to one further report. This would come to light in December 1954, by which time Dr Reginald Mac-Donald too had died. After his death, the doctor's widow Dr Flora MacDonald, was going through some of her late husband's papers, when amongst them she found a letter that appeared to have been written using a mirror, as all the words faced in the wrong direction. While that might have hidden the contents from the casual observer, it wouldn't stop anyone with a mirror from reading them. The letter dated back to 14 November 1915, and appeared to have been written by a guest staying at Lochbuie House while the property was being rented by Sir Stephen Gatty. The letter would eventually find its way into the posses-sion of Alasdair Alpin MacGregor, who would record the contents as follows:

> *Telegrams, Lochbuie.*
> *Loch Buie House,*
> *Station, Oban.*
> *Isle of Mull,*
>
> *N.B.*
>
> 14/11/15
>
> *You will be interested to hear that the dog was both seen and heard last night by Miss White!*
> *The description of which has so horribly upset me that I feel scarcely able to write.*
> *I suppose it served me right for not beleiving* [sic] *you yesterday.*
>
> *In future I shall beleive what you tell me.*
> *L. Chamanyon.*

Very mysterious indeed; it is assumed that it relates to the very same black dog that plagued the doctor's patients.

Interestingly, sightings of the mystery black dog haunting the lower part of Mull seem to have ended, to be replaced - apparently - by sightings of a mysterious black cat. Could it be that the mysterious cat and the black dog are related? Could they both be a manifestation of a daemonic entity that appears to the viewer in whatever form they most expect to see? In the doctor's era, tales of black dogs would have been the flavour of the day, whereas today if you are likely to see an usually large black animal stalking along in the countryside, it is most likely to be attributed to a sighting of a black melanistic leopard. So, who knows what shape it will take in the next century.

Do you want chips with that?

As you have no doubt noticed by now, the Western Isles has played host to more than their fair share of faery dogs - from the hunting hounds of the *Sluagh,* to the death-predicting black dog of Mull. But de-spite all these sights, it is rare to find an account of what they actually eat. Certainly, it is *implied* that if you hear the third warning bark, the monstrous hound will be on your trail and hunting you down for dinner - and you're not going as a guest, but rather as the main course.

But one tale from the isle of Lewis, suggests that the faery dog might have been getting a raw deal being portrayed as a flesh-eater, for there is a particular story that suggests that its diet could have been a lot more vegetarian.

The story was recorded by Alasdair Alpin MacGregor, who was told it by a friend living on Lewis re-

counting the events that had befallen his grandfather, many years before. Like many crofters on the island, he would store his supply of potatoes in a barn for later use. So you can imagine his feelings, when he noticed that his store of prize potatoes was starting to diminish, and he could see no good reason for their tendency to vanish. Concerned that thieving human hands were behind the disappearances, he decided to conceal himself in the barn overnight, to see if he could catch the thief in the act, and perhaps persuade the felon of the error of his ways, with a stout piece of wood or other clobbering implement. Whether the crofter fell asleep during the night, or was just looking in the other direction, he would spend many a night guarding the precious potato store, only to find in the morning that yet more potatoes had gone missing. You can imagine the frustration - night after night - trying to catch the thief, and every night failing.

He never did catch anyone in the act, but one morning he *did* find a clue to the identity of the potato thief, for sticking out of one of the potatoes was a big tooth! As he plucked it from the potato, he could tell that it wasn't from a human; rather it was a dog's tooth, a very big dog's tooth. The crofter was in no doubt as to the owner of that tooth - it had come from a faery dog.

Upon discovering the tooth, there was no further point in staking out the barn. After all, with the faery dog's reputation, would anyone fancy hitting one over the head with a two-by-four, and making it out alive? So it was that the crofter put up with the faery dog's pilfering of his potatoes... but it wasn't *all* bad, because the crofter had been left with something of value out of the whole episode: ownership of a faery dog's tooth. While it might not strike everyone as a bargain, the tooth *did* have its uses. You see, the faery tooth is reputed to have a number of magical properties; for example:

- if your cattle are ailing, and not looking their usual chipper selves, just dip the tooth in a pail of water, get the cattle to drink it, and before you know it they are back to being happy cattle.
- perhaps you think that the local witch has been stealing the goodness from your milk? No problem! The faery tooth puts the goodness back in.

I dare say it would probably be good at piercing cans, and taking the metal tops off beer bottles too. So valuable would this faery tooth be, that it would end up being passed down through the family, and eventually finding its way to Canada with one of the crofter's descendants, where - no doubt - the owner has no trouble with the goodness going from his milk.

One last hound

Before you think that the faery dog is another of those mystery animals that belongs in the far reaches of the dim and distant past, here's a story of a sighting that occurred within living memory - maybe not within the life-span of every reader, but certainly within reach of plenty. The sighting took place in September 1949, when Morag MacCartney - a resident of Greenock - was visiting relatives on the isle of South Uist.

The sighting took place one dark night, close to midnight, when Morag and her cousin were escorting the teacher from Garynamoine back home to the school-house, after they had all spent the evening together at South Boisdale with the rest of Morag's relatives.

So it was in high spirits that the three of them set off into the darkness for the short journey. You may wonder why all three of them set off, for surely no knife-wielding mugger lay in wait just around the corner. It doesn't seem that any member of the party needed to be carried - certainly not Morag, as she is on record as saying that she didn't drink. But real darkness does have its own problems. When it's dark in the country, it really is dark; not like the darkness of many towns and cities today, where the night sky seems to glow orange under the glare of so many street lights. So it was without the benefit of street lighting that the group set off along the road to the school-house, no doubt stumbling along in the darkness, but nevertheless in high spirits, despite the hidden peril that a roadside ditch in the dark offers.

Their route took them along the side of Lochnan Eilean for a short distance, before they crossed the Trossary Burn, and followed the road as it went uphill towards the main road that runs the length of Uist. As the group reached the foot of the incline, Morag would note how dark it was. Normally, you would be able to see the white-painted house that stands halfway up the hillside. Usually, the white structure would reflect the moonlight, and could be used for a directional landmark, but so dark was the night, so devoid of moonlight, that she was unable to see even this local feature. It was a good job that her companions knew the way, or she would have been truly lost that night; blundering around in the dark. But then again, if it had not been for her companions, she wouldn't have been *out* in the dark.

Despite the all-encompassing darkness, Morag became vaguely aware of a white dog some way up the road in front of them. She didn't for one second consider it at all out of the ordinary that a small white dog could be seen, when the large solid house was hidden by the night. As they walked towards the dog, Morag didn't notice anything amiss. Even when it started to run towards them, it only attracted a little of her attention. Only when the dog was very close, did she start to pay more attention to the animal, as it appeared that it was going to run straight into the group. She was, of course, expecting the dog to break to one side and run around them, but much to both her amazement and surprise, it ran straight between Morag and the teacher without touching either of them. Finally the penny seemed to drop, that something unnatural was afoot, and she started to scream in terror; for no dog possessed such talents of self-illumination, or the ability to fit through small gaps. The sudden screaming fair unnerved her two companions, as unlike Morag they had not seen any sign of the white dog that had so terrified her. Worriedly, her companions asked the cause of her distress, as they were oblivious to any reason nearby, and Morag's cries were starting to get to them. Eventually, she was able to tell them what she had seen.

Had they not seen the white dog themselves, she asked. No, they hadn't seen anything, they replied. Surprised by their answer, she explained that as they had started to walk up the incline, she had been aware of a white dog that was about the size of an Arran Collie. And despite the darkness, it had been as easy to see as if it were daylight; so bright was its coat.

She went on to describe the dog; how white it was apart from its small black head, and that its plumy tail curled right over its back. She now realised it was odd that no noise had come from the dog as it raced along, and - with the benefit of hindsight - also strange that as it had run towards them, head down low to the ground. It had given the impression that it was watching the three of them, despite the fact that Morag hadn't actually seen the dog's eyes, or even a reflection from them, hidden as they were under its brow. But even all those unnerving facts, were nothing compared to the horror that she had felt when the dog had run between them. Morag had turned to follow its track, but instead of seeing the white dog running into the distance, there was nothing to be seen; it had completely vanished from sight. Despite her good description, and obvious distress, her cousin and

the teacher still remained sceptical; after all, how could they have missed such a sight, when - according to Morag - the white dog had started off in front of them all.

Eventually things calmed down, and the three of them made it to the school-house at Garynamoine, and left the teacher safely behind, before Morag and her cousin headed back to the house in South Boisdale. This journey was without incident, and Morag and her cousin soon arrived back. It wasn't long before the subject of conversation turned to Morag's unexpected outburst earlier that night. It was her aunt who asked the question: "What did you see then? Was it a white dog?"

It was only then, that Morag discovered that the dog was far from being a natural creature, but something altogether more mysterious. She had had an encounter with the *cu sith*, the faery dog; lucky for her, that it didn't seem to be interested in barking that night, for the chances of running away in the all-prevailing darkness must have been remote.

It would appear that when it comes to sightings of the faery dog, only certain people are able to see it. Only Morag out of the three was so gifted, and it would appear that Dr Reginald MacDonald was another, as his many encounters with the Black Dog of Ardura demonstrates. So, who knows? One day if you're out and about in the Western Isles, and you're one of those people gifted enough to see the *cu sith*, just remember if it starts to bark, you only have two barks in which to find safety, because you really don't want to be within earshot of the third.

BIG CATS

There are many things that have been sighted in the Hebrides that seem out of place, if not downright odd. But when you think about it, tales of sea serpents, mermaids and lake monsters are the kind of things you might expect to see in a chain of islands that not only stretch for hundreds of miles of coastline, but are abundant with both freshwater and sea lochs. But would you *really* expect to find big cats roaming around the islands? Well, the answer is a somewhat surprising yes (or at the very least, a maybe).

While the Scottish wildcat is known to still exist in the north of Scotland, ** it is not widely believed to have made it out to the islands - or if it *did* in fact make it out there, it doesn't seem to have survived to the present day. That said, it has been suggested that something resembling the wild cat has been known to have been sighted around the hills of Uig on the west side, but they could equally be feral cats that have found living in the hills to their liking; but that takes us away from the promised big cats - so on with the story.

As you can imagine, small islands off the west coast of Scotland (no matter how scarcely populated), would make the most unlikely of places for a big cat to live undetected for any length of time. True, there is the tradition of the *Cait sith* - the fairy cat - in the highlands of Scotland. It is said to be the size of a

---

EDITOR'S NOTE: The Scottish wildcat, was for many years seen as a separate subspecies *grampia* of the European wildcat *Felis silvestris*. However, in 2007 DNA analysis suggested that all European wildcats were a single subspecies. *F. s. silvestris*. To confuse the old-school taxonomists even further, several different species have been lumped together: *Felis lybica* (for example) no longer exists as a separate species. Wildcats are now divided into the following subspecies:

Felis silvestris silvestris (Europe and Turkey).
Felis silvestris lybica (North Africa, Middle East and Western Asia, to the Aral Sea).
Felis silvestris catus (Domestic Cat, Worldwide).
Felis silvestris cafra (Southern Africa).
Felis silvestris ornata (Pakistan, north east of India, Mongolia and northern China).
Felis silvestris bieti (China).
Science 27 July 2007: Vol. 317. no. 5837, pp. 519 - 523
The Near Eastern Origin of Cat Domestication

large dog, and jet black in colour, with the exception of some white markings on its chest. But those reports are, on the whole, restricted to the mainland, and since the discovery of the Kellas cat, they have largely been understood to fit the description of that animal.

But the first of a recent run of reports of big cat sightings in the Hebrides turned up in the most unusual of places: the small, but perfectly formed, island of Colonsay. The island itself is just a mere 20 square miles, and hosts a population of around one hundred. Access to the island these days is restricted to ferries from either Oban, around three hours sailing away, or from Port Askaig on Islay, which lies around ten miles to the south, and about an hour's travelling away. Of course, I'm forgetting that there is another closer access point - and that is the Strand, a beach that becomes exposed when the tide is low, and joins Colonsay to the nearby smaller island of Oronsay. Well off the beaten track, the island would therefore seem an unlikely setting for a sighting of a big cat, but one *did* take place on a nice, clear, sunny day in July 1999.

A couple reported that while out walking on Colonsay, they were surprised to stumble across what they would describe as a big cat. The husband was the first to notice it, and soon called his wife across to take a look at the creature. They were standing around 50 yards from the animal, as it stood in front of a stone dyke. They described the cat as being much bigger that a Scottish wildcat, with a body length and height that was comparable with the size of a collie. The body was slim, with a bushy tail, and it had no discernable markings, but rather a dark brown colouring. As the couple watched, they were able to hear it make a loud cat-like yowling sound.

They watched the cat for around 20 seconds, with it seemingly unaware of their presence, before it sprang into life, jumped over the stone dyke, and disappeared into the ferns that lay behind it. Not doubting that they had really seen a big cat, the couple decided to change the route of their walk, and to head in another direction than that which the mystery cat had gone. Later on that day, they would mention the sighting in the local shop-cum-post office, but the girl behind the counter told them that there had been no similar sighting ever reported before, and going off the lack of reports, there have been none since.

It's hard to believe that something such as a big cat would be able to remain hidden on such a small island but then if you are not looking for one would you expect to see one? Of course that still leaves the bigger question of how such a creature would have made it to the island in the first place, certainly it's hard to imagine that it bought a ticket at Oban and just hopped on the ferry.

Rather annoyingly, I wasn't that far away from Colonsay at the time, being on Islay making the most of the good weather, and the empty golden sandy beaches that you find there. I was travelling throughout the Western Isles, and had it not been for a tight deadline, and not being able to catch the ferry from Port Askaig on the Wednesday, I may well have had a sighting of the mystery beast myself. It's certainly a small enough island to have given me a fair chance of one. Of course, while I missed this particular big cat by around ten miles, it reminds me that I had actually come a lot closer to seeing one once before, this time on the Scottish mainland.

Way back in April 1991, long before my interest in mysteries had turned to all things crypto-zoological, I was with my parents in the west coast town of Oban, and while there I missed out on another sighting of a mystery cat. This time I was even closer to the animal, and would have seen it, had I not decided to sit in front of the television with a bottle of beer, rather than to accompany my parents on an early evening walk. As I sat watching the

DRUID'S CIRCLE, COLONSAY.

regional news on TV, they went for a walk along the back of town, and towards Haggarts Brae. Just as they approached said brae, they happened to spot ahead around 60 feet away at the top of a small hill, a large black cat that my mother would describe as being similar to a panther; that description being based on one that she had once seen chained up in a circus in Colywn Bay. And they are the only two occasions that I have known I have been near a big cat. Of course, I have to say that my living in Stornoway, has somewhat limited the opportunities for being so close again, but one lives in hope; after all, you wouldn't think Colonsay was exactly high on the list of places to see one either.

But if Colonsay has just the one sighting, it has to be Mull that holds claim to being the island most likely to harbour a big cat amongst its hills. Mull is a much larger island than Colonsay, and is also a lot closer to the mainland - a couple of miles from the nearest point across the Sound of Mull, but still a long way for a cat to swim. The first recorded sighting there took place back in 1978, and was made by a Mrs. G. W. Brodie while she was on holiday. It took place one morning, as she was driving slowly along at the same time as spotting wild birds (not something that I would recommend). Rather than just spotting birds, Mrs. Brodie and her companion spotted something rather more feline. When she described the sighting in 1985, she would state that at first glance they thought the animal was a black dog; perhaps a Labrador. But then it crossed the road, and started to climb over some rocks heading up to the foothills of Ben More. As it moved, it became apparent that the animal was not a dog after all, but a large black cat. They watched as it covered a distance of 25 to 35 yards, and presumed that the cat was either a panther or other black cat that had been left to fend for itself. They also noted that it seemed to be in very good condition.

It would be over another twenty years before the next flurry of sightings would take place on Mull. The first would occur over the Christmas break, when a couple were driving around the north side of Loch na Keal where they had been filming otters. As they drove along, they became aware of a large cat sitting upon a ridge above the road. They first noticed it as it looked down in their direction. They stopped the car and attempted to stalk the cat, but to no avail - it was having none of it, and quickly moved off into the trees. While they had not been able to get within 50 metres of the animal, the couple would confirm that it was both large and black.

It was only a couple of months later, when the same couple would *again* spot a mystery cat. This time they were on the south side of Loch na Keal, driving along slowly, looking both at the loch for a sight of otters that could be filmed, and equally scanning the sky looking for any sign of eagles. It was while scanning the skyline, that they noticed a black object a long way off in the distance. It was a clear spring day with no shadow, and it was this lack of shadow that sparked their interest. Stopping the car, the occupants would at first attempt to get a view of the creature using their binoculars, but found the magnification wasn't good enough. As luck would have it, the magnification on their camera lens enabled them to see clearly a fairly large black cat in the act of stalking a number of sheep on the hill above, and to the west of it. Despite the cat's best efforts, the lack of cover rather made its attempts at stalking the sheep impossible. Sheep are rather skittish creatures at the best of times, and the sight of a large black cat was no doubt too much for them: they moved off away from it, and in that most feline of ways, the cat just gave up following, and sat up.

Two reports from the area seem pretty extraordinary, but how about a third? This one was made by a group of three people holidaying on Mull in October 2003. The three of them were driving through Gruline heading back from the Ross of Mull at around 3pm. For those who are not familiar with the geography of the isle of Mull, Gruline is to be found at the head of Loch na Keal. Do you see a pattern forming here?

What they reported seeing was an animal that they described as looking like a large cat, which was either very dark or black in colour, that was stalking along the grass verge at the side of the road. From their position, around 150 yards from the mystery animal, they at first thought that it might be a dog, but that idea soon went from their minds when the creature turned sideways on and briefly crouched, before jumping into the nearby trees. It was only when seeing the animal in profile that they were able to identify it as a cat, albeit a very large one. It was far too large to be a domestic cat, no matter how many pies it had eaten, nor did its appearance resemble that of either a dog or a deer. The consensus of opinion was that it appeared to be a puma, basing their description on the Surrey puma that had received extensive coverage in the media.

It would be another few years before the next round of Mull sightings. The first sign of the new wave was a report made to the Big Cats in Britain (BCIB) organisation. The sighting took place early one morning just half an hour after dawn while the reporter was driving to catch the morning's ferry from Craignure. The witness would describe how they had seen a large panther-sized black cat come out of the woodland at a distance of around 100 metres. Despite the distance it became apparent that the cat was far bigger than any domestic cat gone feral as the animal walked past a snow marker pole. For those who are not familiar with these poles, they are to be found along the sides of some roads in the highlands and islands of Scotland, and mark the edges of the road surface when the snow is deep. They are striped, with black and white segments, and it was these coloured segments that would aid the witness in working out the size of the cat, giving the animal a height of three feet at the shoulder. Having seen such a sight, the witness stopped the car and watched the cat walk towards it up to about 60 metres distant, before it once more disappeared into the coniferous woodland.

Bringing the sightings from Mull more up to date, another two reports were made to the BCIB in 2007, the first of these in March. The area was far to the north of the previous sighting, in the vicinity of the island's main settlement of Tobermory. The three witnesses were on holiday and driving along, when they noticed a large black cat walking along the edge of a field into woodland. The witnesses' estimate of the cat was of an animal that was 3 feet long, and 2 feet in height, with a thick tail that was up to 2 feet long, but as the sighting took place at a distance estimated to be up to 500 feet away, it would be difficult be certain of the size.

The final sighting from Mull took place one evening in late May of the same year, on the Torosay Castle Estate, Craignure. The cat spotted on this occasion was described, once again, as being black in colour, and was observed through a pair of binoculars from the opposite end of a field through which it was walking. The witnesses reported that they would compare the cat they saw as being similar in size to the farmer's male collie dog.

One last sighting in 2007 is a little scant on details, but on the 2nd February there was the first report of a mystery big cat on Skye.

It was once pointed out to me that any large black cat is unlikely to be a puma, as such colouring doesn't occur in that species. So any sighting of a big black cat would be more likely to be of a black panther. Of course, one could reply that it is equally as unusual and unlikely for a large cat of *any* colour, be it puma or panther, to be found in the British countryside. But then again, who knows?

So back to Mull: is there one big cat running around Loch na Keal, and another around the Craignure area? Or are they just the visual signs of a small population of mystery moggies on the loose? So if indeed a large cat *has* been seen, the question again has to be where has it come from? Is it just a large domestic cat that has decided to move up from catching the odd mouse, and terrorizing the bird table, to hunting fully grown sheep? It would appear unlikely; it is a fair leap in scale, but could you imagine your cat dropping a dead sheep at your feet as a present, instead of a rather bloody three-legged rodent?

Could the sightings be of either an escaped or deliberately released big cat, that had - until recently - been in someone's private collection? Or at the very least, one that had been kept locked in the shed at the bottom of someone's garden, where no doubt - its nightly growls unnerved the neighbours somewhat. Therein lies one of the problems of the cat having been kept as a pet on a small island: it would be fair to say that everyone and their dog would have known about it. The island location would also suggest that it is unlikely that it would be a release, especially as there is plenty of wide open countryside on the mainland for a big cat to roam, and certainly enough food to keep it going.

Perhaps then, these sightings are of the legendary *Cait sith* going about its business; namely hunting sheep, or could it be something left over from a very dark act that is said to have happened upon this same island, and which goes by the name of the Taghairm? The Taghairm was a dark ritual that was used to call up daemonic entities in order for the attendees to gain wishes from them. It was last reported to have taken place on Mull, the act being described in the *London Literary Gazette* in March 1824, where it was stated that the aim of this Taghairm was to raise the daemonic god of the cats.

This ceremony called for a succession of black cats to be fastened to a spit, one at a time, where each animal was slowly roasted before a fire. Eventually the cat would be roasted to death and another unfortunate animal would take its place to be similarly tortured. This could last for up to four days before a result was achieved. The screams of these dying cats would eventually call forth a number of ghostly cats who joined the pained wailing. The climax of all this cruelty, was when an enormous phantom black cat would appear, and grant the torturer one wish, if they would stop their actions and let the remaining cats go.

And what was the name of that big, black, daemonic, wish-granting cat? It was Big Ears - yes Big Ears, not what you would really expect, is It? It's rather like finding out that the man-eating fearsome tiger that has been terrorizing the Indian village is called Mr. Tiggles. Perhaps it is an echo of that act that has created the mystery big cat of Mull. Then again, it could just be one that has swum out across the sea from Oban.

FUNKY FISH, DANGEROUS MICE AND OTHER CRITTERS

The fearful feolagan

There are many tales of fearsome mystery animals that visit the isles - be they big cats stalking the wild hills around Loch na Keal on Mull, or the massive sea serpents that swim around the channels separating the many islands - but none of these creatures can measure up to anything as bad as the feolagan.

But what is the feolagan? Well, the best description is that it's a bit like a mouse, and a very dangerous one at that, especially if you are a sheep going about your business. It was once said that this tiny animal was responsible for the deaths of many sheep throughout the pastures of the Hebrides, but it was on Lewis, on the hills around Kebock Head, that it was most likely to be found.

You may wonder how an animal that appeared to be just a big mouse could be a danger to sheep. It would appear that the feolagan had the ability to paralyse any sheep that it had the opportunity to come across. Or more correctly, it would paralyse any sheep whose back it was able to run over, for it was the act of walking over the back of the sheep that so affected it. Certainly the prospects for the affected sheep would not look good unless the shepherd was able to catch the very same feolagan that had afflicted his woolly charge and get it to walk over the sheep's back in the opposite direction. This, it seems, would free up the sheep once more.

Eventually someone hit on the smart idea of having a feolagan shaker to cure the sheep of their condition. This worked in the following way, first you would have to catch yourself a feolagan as it ambled on by, then once it had been captured, things went downhill rapidly for the little creature. Let's just say that the dead body of the feolagan would be preserved in a jar containing salt and over time the salts would take on some of the animal's magic so that the next time you happened to find that one of your sheep was incapacitated in the field you would take out your special little salt container and proceed to shake a few grains over the back of your animal. If it turned out the sheep had been paralysed by a run-in with a feolagan, the grains would free the animal up, and it could go on its daft sheep-like way once more. Of course, if the shaker treatment didn't work, then whatever had happened to your sheep hadn't been the result of a run in with a feolagan after all, and your sheep was just buggered.

There's a fish in my pail

These days you take it for granted that if you turn on a tap fresh water will pour out from it, and on the whole, it is quite drinkable. Certainly in some parts the water might look unpleasant, where it takes on the colour of the peat through which it has travelled, but supposedly it's safe enough to drink, although it's probably best not to wash your clothes in the stuff (no matter how good your detergent). And while there might be the odd apocryphal story of the sheep floating in the reservoir, actually thinking about it, that isn't that hard to believe. It's not difficult to find the odd bloated corpse floating about. Still sheep aside, you wouldn't really expect to find anything in your drinking water, but that might just be because it can't fit down the pipes. So these days, most people have forgotten about the old wells, and the tales that go with them.

The isle of Skye had more than its fair share of wells. One, for instance, was known for the qualities of its water, that when consumed alongside strands of dulse (a red seaweed) would sustain the local inhabitants in times when food was otherwise scarce. Luckily, these days, there are supermarkets to be found on the island, so surviving on seaweed and charmed water is no longer a necessity. All very well, you may say, but where is the mystery animal in this story? For that, we need to look in another couple of wells that were to be found further south on Skye.

The animal in question isn't that mysterious. It's a trout, or more correctly, two of them. The mystery is how they ended up in a couple of wells. The first one was to be found in days gone by in the rather aptly named Well of the Trout (it does exactly what it says on the label). It was said that centuries ago it contained a single trout that would happily swim around in the still waters, and would - on occasion - manage to get itself caught in the pail when it was being raised to the surface. Luckily for the plucky fish, on such occasions, it would always find itself being gently lowered back into the waters of the well to go about its business once more. It was a good job the locals weren't faced with starvation, and a diet of seaweed strands, or the story may not have had such a happy ending for the trout. But that wasn't the only well in which a trout could be found. There was also the *Tobar Bhan* (White Well), a well with the tradition that using it would cure any ailments that the locals might have. It was not only the waters that they would partake of, there was also watercress and a herb going by the name of 'flower of the three mountains', which was handy for all those medical needs, and if *that* wasn't good enough, there was also a trout to be found swimming around in its depths.

While so far it seems that these tales of trout-infested wells hark back many centuries, Alasdair Alpin MacGregor, in his book *Peat Fire Flame*, recounts that an old woman going by the name of Anne Mac-Rae used to clean the White Well from time to time, and ensure that gravel from the shore was sprinkled upon its approaches. Not only did she clean the place up, but she also looked after the well-being of the sacred trout. Unfortunately it was noted that with the death of Anne MacRae around the turn of the twentieth century, the trout was to be found no more in the White Well, nor does it appear that there are any further reports of trout to be found hiding in the wells of Skye.

Just how did they get there?

Not every mystery animal that is spotted in the Western Isles is the actual mystery; sometimes the mystery is how it got there. For example, as recently as December 2008, a large bat flying around the skies of South Uist was photographed by Steve Duffield. The bat in the image was a mystery, as it appeared to be too large to be a pipistrelle, one of the species that are to be found in the Western Isles. On a summer's evening, I can watch these bats flying around the garden, and skilful little flyers they are too. But back to the mystery bat of South Uist: opinion was divided as to the type of bat that had been filmed; suggestions being that it was either a noctule or a rarer Leisler's bat. An early theory was that it had been blown off course while migrating in North America, that was until it was suggested that it may have flown in from the mainland. Let's hope it has a longer future than the two bats that were observed being chased by a peregrine falcon over on Skye.

Despite the mystery surrounding the type of bat, it seems likely that it flew to the area but not every odd sighting has the wings to do that kind of thing. For example, take the creature in the next tale: a European brown bear.

We have to go back to August 1980, to find the last sighting of a bear running wild in the Western Isles. But how this 8ft tall, 40 stone beast came to be loose in the Isles is easy enough to explain. Hercules (for that was his name) was a brown bear that had been used in a number of television commercials, and it was while he was filming on location in Benbecula, that Hercules made his bid for freedom. While having a swim, he made the most of the opportunity and headed off for distant shores. Well, maybe not *that* distant. He ended up on the isle of Wiay, which comes in at 930 acres.

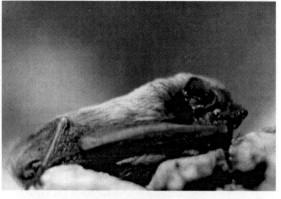

It would be another three weeks before he was tracked down, and recaptured, thanks to a tranquilizer dart, and that - as far as I know - is the only report of a bear running wild in the Outer Hebrides. **

But it certainly makes you think: if something the size of a brown bear can remain hidden on one of the small barren isles of the Hebrides, what other kinds of creatures could be hidden in them elsewhere.

For example, do the hills around Uig on the west side of Lewis still play host to the Scottish wildcat? Certainly they appeared to have done so as late as the 1930s, despite the fact that as far back as 1885, they were deemed to have been extinct on the Western Isles since historic times. This statement is regardless of

TOP: Leisler's bat BELOW: Noctule

the fact that records show that in 1876 thirty wildcats were caught by gamekeepers; of course, these may have been nothing more than feral cats, but it does make me wonder.

Sometimes an unexpected animal swims by, and occasionally the source of the sighting isn't some great sea serpent or fearsome water horse; the nineteenth century saw a couple of walruses swimming in the waters. The first sighting of a walrus took place in 1817, in the vicinity of a herring curing site at Caolas

THE WALRUS, OR SEA-HORSE

** EDITOR'S NOTE: We have one other bear story in our files. Between 1992 and their deaths in 1999 and 2001, we had next door neighbours called Lee and Roly Hollaway, who were keen birdwatchers, and very supportive of what the CFZ stood for. Indeed, I performed the eulogy at Lee's funeral, and Richard and I were with Roly the night he died.

They both told us how, in 1985 whilst on a cycling holiday on Skye, at dusk, they had cycled straight past what looked like a large brown bear rootling about in the undergrowth. As both the witnesses are dead, and there is no further information, this story is included for completeness rather than for any other reason.

Stocnis (Loch Stocnis), and following the traditional response to seeing something unusual in the nine-teenth century, it was killed. At least it didn't have to put up with the ignominy of being stuffed; the re-mains were just lost. A mere twenty-four years later, another walrus would put in an appearance - this time in the region of East Haskeir on the isle of Harris, and sadly its fate wasn't much better than the previous sighting: it was shot by a Captain Macdonald.

If nothing else, they seem persistent these walruses, because 1886 would see a couple of them. The first was made by a Captain Macdonald (whether this is the same Captain MacDonald is not recorded) but the location of the sighting was given as being off Waternish, on the isle of Skye. He observed the animal close to some rocks near Stein, and was sure it was a walrus, after the animal lifted its head, displaying its tusks. Maybe this observer was a *different* Captain MacDonald, because the walrus managed to get away without being shot, which could mean that it was the same animal that would be seen swimming off the coast of Skye a little later. This time, true to form, it would be shot at by a gamekeeper, but for once it appears that the target was missed, as there are no details of the animal being caught.

While the next animal may not seem to be in the same league as any of the above, it's certainly a mystery how it arrived in the Outer Hebrides. And what is this mystery cryptid? Just the little old fox.

The first fox sightings started to appear late in 2005, but it is certainly possible that prior to that date there had been other sightings of foxes that had not been reported. The first of four sightings was in De-cember, when a fox was reportedly seen on a croft at Tolsta on the east side of Lewis. This was soon followed by a sighting at nearby Gress. The final two sightings of 2005 would be mentioned in the local paper, the *Stornoway Gazette*. The first was a report of a fox seen crossing the Barvas road, which does-n't really narrow it down much, as it's quite a long road stretching many miles across from the east to the west side of Lewis. But even that vague report is better than the last one, which mentioned that fox cubs had been seen beside some loch. But as the exact location is not reported, and as there are a few hundred lochs to choose from, it doesn't help pin-point the site.

If the sightings of 2005 had ended up being a little vague, then the first sighting of 2006 would be one of the best, if not *the* best. It took place far to the south of the earlier sightings; so far south, that we have to leave Lewis, and head down to Harris.

It was late on the afternoon of Saturday 18th February, when professional mammal biologist, Dr Sugoto Roy of the Hebridean Mink Project, saw a fox. His sighting was to last for fifteen minutes, as he watched the creature forage near the Urgha-Rhenigidale footpath by the road from Tarbet to Scalpy. The sighting ended when the fox disappeared from view as it headed off to the hills. This particular sighting led to a Scottish Natural Heritage press release issued on 21st February 2006, appealing for more information on the possible spread of foxes on the island, but despite the publicity, it would not be until May of the same year before the next sightings took place.

The first of these would occur back up in Lewis, but this time on the west coast, when a report of fox droppings was made, and it was commented that dogs in the area were acting in a strange manner when confronted with the new smell. The final sighting of the month, would be on the 28th, when a fox was reported to be seen in an unidentified garden somewhere on the island.

You wait a couple of months for a sighting, and then two turn up at once; just like buses these foxes. The next two sightings took place on the islands of Benbecula and South Uist, much further south than any previous ones. The earlier sighting of foxes moving down from Lewis to Harris would have involved a fair bit of walking, but getting down to these two islands would require a good deal of swimming or a ferry ticket. Regardless of how they got there on the evening of 6th June, two sightings occurred, first at Daliburgh, South Uist as the fox crossed the road; and the second sighting that day, took place at Lini-clate, Benbecula. These are - *in theory* - close enough for it to be the same fox, but that isn't to say there couldn't just as easily have been a couple of them.

By the end of June there would also be a report of fox droppings by Garry Bridge at Tolsta but no actual sight of the animal responsible. Still in 2006, August would provide another couple of sightings. Again, these would take place on Lewis. The first report would be a sighting of a fox made on the road somewhere between Gisla and Grimersta, while the last sighting that month would take place on the 31st and would involve a fox seen near a fish farm near to Arnol. Once again, there would be a couple more months with no reports before a further sighting of a fox on a croft in Gress.

The final sighting of a fox to be reported would be in January 2007, when one was seen amongst the trees by the roadside in Aline. After this, it seems that the foxes disappeared from the isles, or at least people have stopped reporting them. Maybe they are just waiting for the opportunity to make a big comeback in 2009. Despite the Harris sighting, it is still the official belief that foxes are not really to be found, which does make you wonder what you would need to confirm a sighting; a body, and eight qualified witnesses perhaps? Well, it would certainly help.

Of course, the question remains: regardless of whether they are still to be found here, just how did they manage to get out to the Outer Hebrides? It's easy enough to see how the bat could have flown to South Uist. After all, they have the technology in the shape of wings. It is also possible to see how the wildcat could have hidden out in the more remote parts of the island. If you are not of interest, you soon disappear from view. The walruses - of course - were able to swim down to the Western Isles under their own steam; not like it did them any good! Of course, the foxes could have followed the bear's approach, and thumbed a lift.

The King Otter

There is a tradition of a certain kind of otter that is said to haunt the waters of the Western Isles. Back in the seventeenth century Martin Martin would write about this animal, and he christened it with the name that it is known by today: the king otter.

This otter was far bigger than its contemporaries, as befits a creature of the standing of a king in the animal kingdom. It could be identified not only by its large size, but by the white spot - no bigger than the size of an old sixpence (slightly larger than the size of a modern five pence piece) - that appeared upon its breast (something it shares with the faery cat, the *cait sith*). If that wasn't a big enough clue to the animal being a king otter, there was also the group of seven smaller otters that would accompany it at all times. ** Whether it is still to be found today is hard to say, as even at the time Martin was writing about it, he described it as being a rare animal that was seldom seen. And what reason could there be for its rarity? Well, it was worth hunting.

The reason that the king otter was worth hunting was its skin. Not for it to be used as a fashion accessory but rather because tradition had it that the pelt of the king otter had special magic powers, and it was those powers that made it valuable. So valuable was the skin that it was said to be worth more that the number of guinea coins than it would take to cover it completely.

** EDITOR'S NOTE: This is a remarkable piece of synchronicity, because another mystery aquatic carnivore has been reported to do exactly the same thing. However, this one is found on the opposite side of the Atlantic Ocean. Here is an excerpt from p.30 of the CFZ Guyana 2007 Expedition report:

Whilst we waited at Point Ranch, I asked about the water tiger. An old man called Elmo, who came from the ranch, had seen them. He was adamant that they were not the giant otter (Pteronura brasiliensis) with which he was familiar. Elmo said that the water tigers he had seen were spotted like a jaguar (Panthera onca) but hunted in a pack. He said that there was a 'master', possibly a parent, that sent out the cubs ahead of it in order to flush out prey. He had seen a whole group of them several years ago. Elmo pointed out a local mountain where he said that a pack of water tigers lived. The mountain had no name, but it was said that a dragon guarded a spring there, and Elmo added that no-one who had ever climbed it had returned.

But what was the power the skin held? Well, according to tradition, it was immune to the weapons of men. That was, however, with the exception of the white spot, which was the only area vulnerable to the huntsman. But he had to be a good shot, because if he missed the vulnerable area it was rumoured to have fatal consequences for the hunter. Even if you *did* hit the right spot, it was said that the killing of a king otter would foretell the death of either a man or a dog. I wonder how many dogs were shot straight after the slaying of a king otter, just to cheat the prophesy of its human victim.

Of course, once you had managed to get hold of your king otter skin you had it made, because you no longer needed to fear injury from arrow, sword, or bullet. Such was the belief in this fact that many of the men from the isles who followed Bonnie Prince Charlie during the Jacobite Rebellion, carried a piece of king otter skin about their person as a way of protection. It was said that many a man came back to the isles from the defeat at the battle of Culloden thanks to that magical piece of skin that had protected them even as the air whistled with the sound of musket balls flying by, and as great clods of earth were sent flying by the many cannon balls raining out of the sky to rest amongst the Jacobite ranks.

Perhaps the king otter is extinct today in the Western Isles. This would be a great pity, for surely there would be less need now for the ballistic protection that its skin offered. Even if it is extinct here, perhaps it lives on in Ireland, as the equally mysterious *dobhar-chu*.

The Killer Deer of Rùm

Rùm - measuring roughly 9 miles by 9 miles - is the largest of the small islands that are to be found to the south of Skye, just 10 miles from the coast of the Scottish mainland. Since 1957 the island had been a National Nature Reserve, home not only to rare plant species, but also to a number of mammal species, with around 200 wild goats on the island. That may sound a fair number of goats, but their number is thrown into the shade by the 1,400 red deer that are also to be found on the island. These are the descendants of animals reintroduced to Rùm after the original native red deer had been hunted to extinction. But it is neither the plants nor the land mammals that are Rùm's main claim to fame; its real treasure are the birds that are to be found there. It was here that saw the shooting of the last native white-tailed sea eagle early in the twentieth century, and it was also one of the sites for the reintroduction of the species when sea eagles from Norway were released here. As impressive as the sea eagle is, the star attraction is what is classed as one of the world's largest colonies of Manx shearwaters - with an estimated breeding population of around 100,000 pairs to be found nesting upon the hills. Spending most of their year out at sea, travelling as far as the waters of Brazil, they return north to breed each March.

It was noticed a few years ago that something was killing the shearwater chicks, and not just killing them, but decapitating them. Just what was responsible for this hideous crime? While the island does have a small population of brown rats, they did not appear to be responsible, so what could the mystery head-hunting beast be?

Well, if you noticed the title of this section you will have a pretty good clue. It turns out that the fearsome head-hunter is none other than the usually harmless and vegetarian red deer (well, they want you to *think* that they are harmless).

For a while, it had been noticed that at the end of each summer a number of headless shearwater chicks would be found near the nesting

sites. Each one would be missing just its head, which hardly fitted into the pattern of predation by crows, eagles or rats. Eventually, those studying the phenomenon received a big clue to what was going on, when a deer-hunter observed a red deer munching upon a chick. From then on the game was up, and the search turned to why these normally harmless animals were coming out on bright nights for a quick nibble of their feathered neighbours.

While, of course, at first this predation by a herbivore would seem to be unique to the deer of Rùm, it was soon being compared to the sheep of the island of Foula in the Shetland Isles, where it was noticed that they also had taken a liking to eating birds, and had been observed eating unfledged Arctic tern chicks. Was this the start of a B-movie plot, where normally harmless herbivores find a taste for flesh; "Birds today, People tomorrow?" Luckily, that doesn't seem to be the case. From observation both the deer of Rùm and the sheep of Foula seem to be fussy eaters, the deer only bite the head off, and the sheep were seen to flip the chicks over so as to bite their legs off. It appears that the wicked ruminants were only interested in the crunchy bits. As they don't seem interested in any other part of the chick, it is suspected that their choice in morsels is the clue to the reason for them eating the birds; both the head and legs contain a concentration of calcium. It appears that the red deer of Rùm have learnt a way to compensate for a shortage of calcium in their diet, which is the result of the mineral poor soils of Rùm, and every self-respecting stag knows that you need to have plenty of calcium if you are to grow a fine set of antlers to impress the ladies.

Let us hope that the race for bigger and better antlers doesn't turn these normally harmless animals into man-killers. It's bad enough having to keep an eye on the ponies to ensure that they are not really an *each-uisge* let alone having to worry about the man-eating deer.

Terrible worms

Of the many mystery animals that have been noted in the region the gigelorum is easily the smallest, and probably the least likely to be found. One reason its discovery is so unlikely, is that the animal is reputed to be very small. In fact - according to the Reverend J. Gregson Campbell who noted its existence - it is reputed to be small enough to build its nest in the ear of a mite. Of course, some people maintain the reason why the gigelorum is unlikely to be found is because it is just made up, but who am I to judge that one?

But the gigelorum isn't the only small creature that was once to be found in the area. There was one other small critter of which reports have disappeared in recent years. In fact, its heyday seems to have been in the 1690s, but even so, it can still send a shiver down the spine. Known as either the fiollan or fillan worm - by either name it was a creepy critter.

Hard to think that a worm could cause such worry in a land where the faery dogs stalk along the lonely lanes and beaches; animals so dangerous, that even their footprints (if stepped in) could lead to madness. And not forgetting that going too close to any number of lonely lochs could call up a visitation from the dreaded *each-uisge,* which threatened to drag you into the dark, still waters and feast upon your drowned corpse (until only your liver was left to float ashore, leaving it as the only physical proof to mark your unearthly demise). And it wasn't as if the seas around the islands offered any respite. If it wasn't the blue men trying to drag you down under the waves of the Minch on the east side of Lewis, then it could be the Gallan Whale feeding on an endless supply of fishermen. And who knows how many people got a little too close to a sea serpent to find out if they really are man-eaters.

So what, you ask, was so special about the fiollan worm? Well, let me enlighten you.

It was Martin Martin who first wrote about the little worm that lived between the flesh and skin. He tells of a boy of around ten years of age, who was living on Skye in the seventeenth century. One day, the boy was mysteriously taken ill; suffering from a pain that travelled from one part of his body to another. As it travelled around the body, numerous bruises started to appear, and his skin turned blue. The boy suffered greatly as the pain moved around; flaring up in his toes, then his thighs and testicles before moving on to his arms, and finally his head.

The poor lad could find relief only by bathing in warm water, but even that wouldn't last for long before the pain started once more. But relief eventually came when the pain and bruising appeared on his head. Spotting some swelling at the back of his head, and observing some movement under the skin, a local woman decided to force out the badness. With her grime-encrusted nails, she endeavoured to remove whatever was lurking below the skin, and after a little squeezing and brushing with her nails, her efforts were rewarded when she forced out a little creature only around an inch in length, and about as wide as a goose quill. The small animal possessed a sharp head that was white in colour, while the red body supported a row of little feet either side that enabled the creature to crawl around the boy's body between the skin and the flesh, causing such pain. She recognized the little animal in her hand as being the dreaded fiollan worm, which at the time, was known to be affecting several other people on the island. On those people it could be seen crawling around the head and legs.

But it wasn't only on the isle of Skye that you had to watch out for this creepy little parasite, for there was a tradition of the fiollan worm being found throughout the rest of the Hebrides. On Harris it was believed that scrofula was as a result of a visitation from this tiny creature. It was said that the worm could be drawn out of the victim by applying a hot fomentation to where it was believed to be lurking beneath the skin. But this would only be of use if the worm's presence could be detected before it had a chance to lay its eggs. Once its eggs were laid, it would be too late for the poor victim, who would soon suffer from many more fiollan worms crawling around his or her body between the skin and the flesh.

Of course, if the eggs were about to hatch, and you couldn't find a pair of willing grubby fingernails to force the worm out, you could always try repeating the following charm; there's no guarantee that it would do any good, but it might take your mind off the feeling of something small crawling below the skin, at least while the bath filled with hot water.

'Death chant of the black worm
Death chant of the evil worm
Death chant of the wasting worm
Of the many feet'

MERMAIDS

The Babe of Benbecula

Benbecula has certainly had more than its fair share of strange things over the years, especially when you compare the size of the place to the long island (Lewis and Harris). From its globsters and faery dogs, to the sneaky Hebridean fox. But perhaps its most celebrated tale is that of the mermaid, although possibly that claim could just as likely be made for the tale of the flight of Bonnie Prince Charlie in 1746, but while that tale may have plenty of adventure and cross-dressing, it isn't for *this* book of mystery animals.

Our tale takes place eighty-four years after Charles's visit, in or about the summer of 1830, off the coast at Sgeir na Duchadh near Grimnis. At the end of a long day of back-breaking seaweed cutting, a group of locals were getting ready to return from the beach to their black houses. One of the women in the group headed down to the lower end of the reef, from which they had been collecting the seaweed, to wash her feet. As she finished, and was about to put her stockings on, she was surprised to hear a splash in the calm sea. Intrigued, she looked around to see what had caused the disturbance. Upon raising her head she was somewhat shocked to see a creature that she could only describe as looking like a miniature woman, swimming just a few feet away. Understandably, this wasn't something that you saw every day, not even in the rather mystery-haunted land that was nineteenth-century Benbecula.

Her stockings now completely forgotten, the woman called out to the rest of the group '*maighdean nan tonn*' - a name translating as 'maiden of the waves' - in other words, a mermaid. Whatever she said, it didn't take long for the rest of the seaweed-cutters to be drawn to the spectacle of the little lady playing in the water, seemingly oblivious to the attention being paid to her. But then again, when have mermaids ever really been the shy, retiring types? Even this demure one was observed to be performing somer-saults, hardly failing to draw attention to herself. Eventually she settled down calmly, to comb her hair in front of the gathered group. Well, if you're a temptress of the deep, it's probably best to look after your hair because you never know who might be watching.

But like the mermaids of the old seafarers' tales, this one was a temptation - no doubt all that hair combing, and not forgetting the topless cavorting which goes with it. What-ever the attraction, a number of the men in the group decided that they would attempt to get a little closer, and try - if possible - to catch the creature. But even as they waded into the cold water out towards her, she would drift just a little further from reach - still playing around - still enticing the men further out. Perhaps that old mermaid gene was kicking in. Regardless of the depth of the water, the men continued to wade in after her. Back on the

beach, the crowd was starting to grow a little larger, as the village children joined in to see the commotion.

Now, while the men of the group may have been prepared to wade and swim out after the mermaid, and the women folk might have been prepared to just stand by and watch them drown; the local children had other ideas. It seems that the good folk of Benbecula had raised a batch of 'Neds' (Non-education Delinquents; a rather delightful Scottish term for youthful wastrels with a little too much time on their hands). For they weren't fooled by the mermaid's glamour, and just followed their natural instincts, no doubt fortified by the odd bottle of Buckie (that's Buckfast Tonic Wine, to the uninitiated; the tipple of choice for those who require cheap strong alcohol), they just picked up some of the large pebbles that littered the beach, and started to throw them at the cavorting mermaid.

Perhaps because she was spending all her time teasing the men, she wasn't aware of the new threat that was flying through the sky towards her. The majority of the stones splashed harmlessly in the sea around her - some overshooting, some falling well short - but one of the stones must have had Goldilocks's name on, because it was just right (if not deserved). That one stone struck the mermaid in the back, and as if pole-axed, she slipped below the waves, no doubt to the annoyance of the pursuing men. And if you think about it, the mermaid probably wasn't all that impressed either. It was probably a good job for the Neds that it was a west coast merbeing, because if it had been one of the east coast blue men, they would have probably been throwing the stones back; much rougher creatures, them, but that's another tale.

Their fun over, the group went back to their seaweed cutting, no doubt discussing what they had been privileged to see. Well maybe the children went off to sup some more Buckie, and hang around to await the introduction of the bus shelter.

If that wasn't mystery enough, the tale takes on a darker tone when - a few days later - a body was washed ashore at Cuile, near the township of Nunton, a couple of miles from where the mermaid had been sighted happily playing.

Now, if you are an old romantic, you might like to think that the body washed up had nothing to do with the mermaid that had been seen playing so happily in the sea near the seaweed cutters. After all, plenty of things wash up on the shore as it is, without the need to add to the list a recently and recklessly killed mermaid. Perhaps the stone only annoyed her, and she had just gone off in a huff. If that's what you prefer to think, fair enough; a happy ending to the story.

If, however, you don't believe in the coincidence of a mermaid being sunk by a stone, and a completely different woman with a tail being washed up on a nearby beach, the rest of the tale might be of interest.

So it was a couple of days later, a bedraggled body was washed up on the shore with the tide. During the day following the first sighting, word had certainly gotten around the area, and there was no doubt that this was the poor unfortunate mermaid, who only a few days before, had been seen splashing around, until her cavorting was stopped by a well aimed rock in what was certainly a terminal way.

Word of the body got round, and reached the keen ears of the sheriff of the district, the baron-bailie and the factor for Clan Ranald, Mr. Duncan Shaw. By the time Duncan Shaw turned up at the scene, a large crowd had gathered around the prone body of the mermaid, no doubt attracted by stories of the early antics of the Babe of Benbecula.

Recording these events seventy years later, Alexander Carmichael, in his book *Carmina Gadelica,* described what the crowd found lying dead at their feet.

'The upper portion of the creature was about the size of a well fed child of three or four years of age, with an abnormally developed breast. The hair was long, dark and glossy, while the skin was white, soft and tender. The lower part of the body was like a salmon, but without the scales. Crowds of people, some from long distances, came to see this strange animal, and all were unanimous in the opinion that they had gazed on the mermaid at last'

When Sheriff Duncan Shaw arrived at the scene, he ordered that the mermaid be given a proper burial; after all, it was the *least* that the community could do after having killed her. So it was that the mermaid ended up being dressed in a shroud, and placed in a small coffin that had been made for her. Once all this had been done, the body was moved a little further inshore from where it was found, and buried; there was even a good turn-out for the impromptu funeral - whether they were there as genuine mourners, out of shame, or just morbid curiosity, we may never know.

But the story doesn't end there, because since that date people have been trying to find this body; possibly the best proof that mermaids are real. That is, it *would* be the best evidence if anyone could find the remains. When Carmichael was writing in 1900 he stated that there were still people alive who had been lucky enough to both see and even touch the mermaid. But as time went on those people eventually died, and the location of the burial site started to be forgotten. Even as late as the 1960s, visitors could still be pointed to the grave of the mermaid in the graveyard at Nunton.

It was in this burial ground, the graveyard of the chapel of St Mary, that the author R. MacDonald Robertson claims to have seen the location of the grave. As the graveyard is east of Cuile Bay it would lend itself to the belief that this *could* be the final resting place, especially if the locals gave the mermaid a Christian burial.

But as it is with these things, there are plenty of other people with different ideas of the final resting place.

In March 1994, Dr Shelagh Smith from the Royal Museum of Scotland, discovered what appeared to be a headstone in the sand dunes at Cuile Bay. This led to the archaeologist Adam Welfare, in August of the same year, to study the stone only to decide that it wasn't a headstone after all. It's recorded that a MacPhee told that his family had a traditional belief that the lifeless body of the mermaid had been washed ashore at the south of Cuile Bay, on a rocky inlet known as Bogha mem Crann (stinky bay); so called as it is a place where fermenting seaweed gathers.

The latest attempt to find this missing vital clue was as recently as 2008, when the American cryptozoologist Nick Sucik spent a few weeks on the island investigating the story. He found a grave-shaped mound in a field that - according to some of the locals - could be the fabled burial site. So far, no digging has taken place. But who knows? It might not be long before we have a firm answer as to what washed up on that beach all those years ago.

But in the continued absence of the body, let's speculate on what it could have been. It is worth considering that the people living in the area would be well versed in the sea creatures to be seen locally, and they would certainly be well able to spot the difference between the washed up remains, and those of say a seal or an otter, so could it be that it really *was* a mermaid?

Of course, there is one other possibility that has struck me since I first heard the story: what if the body they found wasn't the same creature as the mermaid that had been spotted by the seaweed cutters, but rather, a fake.

Now, it is not impossible that at the time there was someone living on Benbecula who had sailed overseas, a long way from the island, and before returning may well have had the opportunity to purchase a Jenny Haniver, a composite mermaid produced for the man who has everything. So hearing the tale, he takes a trip down to the beach one morning, and leaves the 'mermaid' where it can be easily found. With the tales of the recently sighted mermaid still fresh, two and two are added together and hey presto!

But that would just spoil the story wouldn't it? And I look forward to the day when that grave is finally discovered, and the answer finally found, and I for one hope the Babe of Benbecula is a real *maighdean nan tonn*.

Throw her a fish

Sometimes the tales of mermaid sightings in these parts do make you wonder what exactly was going on. There was the tale recorded by Alasdair Alpin MacGregor in *Peat Fire Flame* of a story told by a shepherd living in South Uist to a friend of MacGregor's identified as being John Wilson Dougal of Edinburgh. The tale the shepherd told was said to concern events that had happened just twenty years before. Two fishermen had been hauling in their net, expecting to find nothing other than fish flapping about in it, so imagine their surprise when they discovered a baby mermaid trapped in it. They didn't have long to wonder what to do with the fish-tailed infant, as all of a sudden, the mother mermaid appeared, bobbing up and down in the water next to the little fishing boat. Understandably, she pleaded with the two men for the release of her baby, promising the pair that if they released the child, neither of them would ever have to fear drowning. Whether this 'no need to fear drowning' was a promise or a thinly veiled threat is, even today, open to debate. Threat or not, the question that stuck in the shepherd's mind every time he told the tale was, how come the mermaid spoke Gaelic?

The shepherd's tale is not the only story involving mermaids and their powers concerning drowning. There is the tragic tale of Donald Macleod, a fisherman who hailed from the isle of Mull. MacLeod was part of the fishing crew that went herring fishing one morning out of Loch Boisdale, on the east side of

South Uist. That morning's fishing had been very successful, and it had not taken long for the nets to fill to the brim,
and it was soon time to haul them aboard and begin the
journey back to port. They were soon racing back, helped
on their way by a strong wind that had picked up behind
their boat. It was on this return leg of the journey that one of
the crew noticed that they had company; for there, behind
the boat, a mermaid had appeared.

It didn't take long for the news to spread around the crew.
At first they were nothing more than surprised at their fol-
lower. Despite the fact that the wind was blowing strongly
behind them, and the sails on the boat were straining as the
vessel raced along through the waves, no matter how fast
they moved, the mermaid kept pace behind the boat, and
this soon started to unnerve the crew. The skipper decided
on a course of action; each member of the crew was to
throw a herring to the mermaid, perhaps as a form of ap-
peasement. The skipper was first to throw his herring towards the mermaid, and it landed next to the creature, who
stayed in her position behind the boat, still keeping up with
it, as it headed towards the shore. Each crew member took
their turn to throw a fish to the mermaid, and every time
there was no reaction, that was until it was Donald's turn to
throw a herring. When *his* fish hit the water, the mermaid turned her back on the fishing boat, and dived
below the waves, not to be seen again. Whether Donald's fish had hit her or not is not recorded; it appears that she had just had enough.

Any thoughts of the mermaid's disappearance signifying anything special did not appear to strike Donald
at the time. But when the fishing boat was tied up in the harbour, and the fish were being divided up and
the crew being paid off, the skipper took Donald aside to have a quiet word with him. The information
that the skipper passed onto Donald could not have been of any comfort, for he was told that the mermaid's vanishing act could only mean one thing and that was that Donald was destined to drown one
day. Whether Donald believed this or not is hard to say, but the fact that he didn't venture off the island
for a whole year afterwards suggests one of two things; either he took the warning very seriously, or the
rest of the fishing crews had heard of the incident, and decided that it was better not to have such a
cursed man amongst them. For surely if he was destined to drown, it was better not to be on the same
boat when it foundered and sank, for what guarantee was there of their own survival.

But shortly after a year had passed, Donald Macleod had his chance to set sail once more courtesy of a
man named Duff. Duff was a merchant who operated his business out of Orosay, Castlebay, on the isle
of Barra. He had arrived in Loch Boisdale hoping to buy a boat with the intention of sailing up to Loch
Skipport, South Uist. The merchant was in luck in finding a boat, as the local innkeeper was selling his
boat the *Duffac*. It didn't take long for Duff to become the new owner; now all he needed was a crew and
it was then that he found an idle seaman who fitted the bill - Donald Macleod.

Not knowing anything of Donald's run-in with the mermaid, Duff was happy to hire him for the trip. The
day soon came when the pair set off in the *Duffac* heading for Loch Skipport. It wasn't long after they
had set off that the weather started to take a turn for the worse, but nothing too bad it seemed. The boat
soon left Loch Boisdale, and was last seen by the lighthouse keeper at the Uishnish lighthouse, who
watched its progress through his binoculars. He kept an eye on its progress until it was a mile distant to
the south west of Uishnish, but eventually he had other tasks to attend to, and he put down his binoculars
and headed away from the viewing platform. And that was the last sighting that anyone had of the *Duffac*
and its crew. Had the mermaid come to claim Donald Macleod that day?

Where's my coat? I'm leaving.

Not all the folk found to be living in the waters around the Western Isles are necessarily mermaids, and the Minch may contain more than just the blue men, for old stories tell of the seal folk.

The seal folk resemble seals most of the time, but they have the ability to peel off their seal skin, and take on human form. This they would do in the evening to allow them to dance and cavort on whichever lonely beach took their fancy. How these seals came to have such a strange ability seems to have been lost in the tracks of time. One old tradition hints that a person who drowned in those waters became a seal person, while a version from Iceland suggests that they are formed from an Egyptian pharaoh and many of his soldiers, who drowned when their pursuit of Moses was curtailed by the Red Sea closing over them. Whatever the cause, the results were the same: the drowned individual would be destined to return as either a seal man or woman, depending on their initial gender. As you can see this belief in seal folk is not just restricted to the Western Isles, with similar stories being told as far a way as Iceland, while a little closer in Orkney they are known as the Selkie.

A slightly BDSM depiction of the capture of a seal-woman on a stamp from the Faroe Islands

One seemingly universal tale crops up time and again, and while over the years seal folk have been found in various locations around the world, this version - as you would expect - comes from the Western Isles, in this instance from the isle of North Uist.

Long ago a man going by the name of MacCodrum was walking along the shoreline one evening, and as he walked he became aware of a commotion up ahead of him. Curious to see what was happening, he hurried towards the sound, and on getting close he hid in the dunes. He peered down to see a group of seals on the beach, and as he watched, much to his surprise, they started to unpeel their seal skins to reveal that inside each was a woman. It might have been a voyeur's dream come true, but what MacCodrum made of the scene as he watched the naked women walk into the sea to wash, is not hard to guess. Because as soon as the last of the seal women waded in amongst the breakers, he was up like a shot and down to the beach where he grabbed the first discarded seal skin he could find, and with it trailing behind him, he ran all the way home. He was, of course, well versed in the tradition that if you acquired the skin of a seal woman she would be unable to return to the sea, and could therefore be persuaded to be his wife, which - in the days before mail-order brides - came in handy for lonely men. As soon as MacCodrum was inside his house, he set about hiding the seal skin above the lintel of his doorway. No sooner had he finished doing this, than there was a knock upon the door. On opening it, he wasn't too surprised to find a naked woman standing there - after all, he had only just stolen her skin. He invited the poor seal woman in, and provided her with some women's clothes, (you *do* have to wonder where he got them from. Perhaps he stole those on another evening's walk).

Despite the rather strange start to the relationship, things seemed to work out for the pair, and they soon married, and had many children. While things might have seemed rosy for MacCodrum, his seal wife saw things differently - never forgetting that she was really nothing more than a prisoner in his house, and she would take advantage of every occasion MacCodrum was away from home, to search for the seal skin. Eventually it happened that she came across the secret hiding-place above the lintel, and her long-hidden seal skin. No sooner had she found it than she was running back down to the beach with it, and after a quick change of skins, she was straight into the sea once more; free at last.

A similar tale is told concerning the MacPhees of Colonsay, one of whom discovered a seal skin left on the rocks one day and ran off home with it. Of course, this tale ends with the same conclusion - when the seal woman finds her skin, and races back off to her watery home. While that story might be nothing unusual, the next one - also concerning the MacPhees of Colonsay - has a nice bit of role reversal.

It came to pass one day that one of the MacPhee men was captured by the seal folk, and found himself confined to a sea cavern - for all purposes, the property of a seal woman. While most of his needs were met, there was one thing missing from his life - his freedom. Unlike a captive seal woman he didn't need to find his skin before making a bid for freedom - all he required was an opportunity when he wasn't being watched. Eventually that day came, and MacPhee made the most of it, and was soon back on Colonsay racing back to his home. He needed to move fast, as the seal woman was close behind, (it appeared that she was a little on the possessive side). It was lucky for MacPhee that he happened to be the owner of a particularly big and fearsome black dog; so fierce was this dog, that over the years many of his neighbours had urged him to get rid of the beast as it was far too dangerous - being almost uncontrollable. But every time his neighbours urged him to dispose of the dog, MacPhee would tell them, "The black dog's day is yet to come." Whether he truly believed that is hard to say, but the day of his escape turned out to be that very day of which he had talked.

MacPhee was just short of his house when the seal woman finally caught up with him. But before she could start to carry him back to the undersea cavern, the black dog of MacPhee made its timely appearance, instantly attacking the seal woman. In the ensuing confusion, MacPhee made good his escape, while behind him the seal woman and the black dog fought each other to the death, with the dog killing the seal woman and the seal woman killing the dog. So, in a way, it all worked out in the end; MacPhee regained his freedom and his neighbours finally saw the last of his big black dog.

The Blue Men of the Minch

While they might throw stones at the mermaids down in Benbecula, and even marry them in Orkney, the blue men of the Minch were a different kettle of merfolk altogether.

Today the Shiant Isles are better known for their colonies of seabirds that nest there, and the 3,000 black rats (*Rattus rattus*) that inhabit the island. A now rare species, which are better known for their role in spreading many a deadly plague around in the Middle Ages. But those days are long gone and today those particular rats are only to be found in a few locations around the United Kingdom, and they are no longer the terror they once were. But the Shiants have their own terror in the form of the blue men.

The islands lie four miles off the east coast of the isle of Lewis, and are separated from it by the Sound of Shiant (try saying that when drunk), the stretch of sea known for its turbulent waters. It is the constant stream of blue men swimming around the island, and along that channel that keeps the sea a-churning.

It is said that these human-sized mermen, with their blue caps and grey faces, are to be seen swimming around the Shiant Isles in summer, where they skim just below the surface. But when the seas turn stormy, and the wind howls across the waves, they appear at the surface with their long arms waving, and their heads held erect, as they float waist-high above the waves, spying out the surrounding waters. And when they dive they are described as doing so in a way reminiscent of a porpoise.

The legend goes as follows....

When not swimming around the isles, the blue men resided in caves deep down in the Minch, only a few of them appearing above the water and keeping an eye out for passing vessels. When a ship was sighted, a messenger would swim down, deep to those caves to arouse the rest of the blue brethren, and bring them to the surface to bring misfortune to the ship. If the weather was already stormy, and the ship was struggling, they would gather around and frolic and laugh as the boat slipped below the waves, taking its crew to a watery grave. If the blue men didn't think the ship was sinking fast enough, they would offer a helping hand, before attacking the vessel with their fists, smashing its timbers to pulp.

Should the vessel have survived the attention of both the waves and their fists, the blue men had one further trick up their sleeves to destroy it. The chief of the blue men would rise to the surface, and challenge the boat's captain to a duel consisting of verse recital. If the chief was successful, the prize would be that his followers would seize hold of the boat, upsetting it, and sending it (and the crew) crashing to their doom.

The challenge would consist of two lines of verse which the captain had to answer immediately if death were to be avoided. The transcript of such a challenge has been recorded in Donald Alexander Mackenzie's *Wonder Tales from Scottish Myth and Legend*.

'❒ one day, when the wind was high and the billows rough and angry, the blue men saw a stately ship coming towards their sea-stream under white sails. Royally she cleft her way through the waves. The sentinels called to the blue fellows who were on the sea floor, and as they rose they wondered to see the keel pass overhead so swiftly. Some seized it and shook it as if to try their strength and were astonished to find it so steady and heavy. It carried on straight as a spear in flight.

The chief of the blue men bobbed up in front of the ship and when waist high among the tumbling waves, shouted to the skipper

> 'man of the black cap, what do you say
> As your proud ship cleaves the brine'

No sooner were the words spoken than the skipper answered

> 'my speedy ship takes the shortest way,
> And I'll follow you line by line'

This was at once an answer and a challenge, the chief of the blue men cried angrily

> 'my men are eager, my men are ready
> To drag you below the waves'

The skipper answered defiantly in a loud voice

> 'my ship is speedy, my ship is steady,
> If it sank it would wreck your caves'

The chief of the blue men was worsted. Never before had a seaman answered him so promptly and so well. He had no power to injure the ship, because the skipper was as good a bard as he was himself, and he knew that if he went on shouting half verses until the storm spent itself the skipper would always complete them. He signalled his followers to dive and they all vanished down below the wave ridges, like birds that dive for fish.'

There is also the tale of how one blue man was caught while sleeping upon the surface, by two fishermen. Between them, they managed to drag the sleeping merman onto the boat, and firmly bound him in rope. Once certain that they had their captive secure they made great haste for the shore expecting at any moment to receive attention from other blue men. They hadn't gone far before their worst fears were realised, as a couple of the fellows appeared beside the boat, and began issuing their challenging verse.

> 'Duncan will be one, Donald will be two
> Will you need another ere you reach the shore'

The skipper of the boat knew that he must answer with his own verse, but before he could utter a line, the sleeping captive awoke, and snapped the ropes holding him as if they were nothing but straw. No sooner was he free of his bonds, that he leapt high out of the boat back into the sea, and as he went he gave the last two lines to the verse:

> 'Duncan's voice I hear, Donald too is near,
> But no need of helpers has strong Ian More'

No doubt thinking better of it, the fishermen made for the shore, glad to have escaped the clutches of the blue men.

But what are these blue men? Some would have you believe that the stories are folk tales passed on through the vaguest memories of North African traders, out looking for slaves, or even those angels cast out of heaven that didn't fall quite as far as some.

Yet More Mermaids

Just when you think there are no more to come, another one turns up. You could say mermaids are like buses, but most would say that they are more like topless women with fishy tails, or should that be fishy tales of topless women? Well, they certainly are not a big red bus, *that's* for sure.

Already we have made the acquaintance of the tragic Babe of Benbecula, and the altogether slightly more sinister blue men, so let's round off with another couple of tales. I promise that's it (well, that is if I don't come across any more before I finish writing).

So let's make our first stop on the tiny island of Barra. Just eight miles by four, it's one of the smaller islands in the Outer Hebrides, and sits at the end of the chain. Today its main claim to fame is that its runway could fairly be described as a beach, which in actual fact it is but only when the tide is out. And planes aren't the only things that you find on the beach when the sea goes out - sometimes it's a lass with a tail.

The following tale first turned up in Alexander Carmichael's *Carmina Gadelica,* published over a hundred years ago, so it's fair to say that the event certainly happened a while back.

So it was that one day a crofter from Ceanntangbhal, Barra, going by the name of Colin Campbell, was walking along the beach. As he headed towards the reef at 'Caolas Cumhan', he caught sight of something sitting on the reef. As he moved a little closer he was certain that what he could see was an otter sitting there holding a fish between its paws as if about to eat it. Like the majority of the gun-toting locals we have met so far, his first thought was to shoot it (well at least it wasn't the last great auk). Steadying himself, Colin raised his gun and started to take careful aim; after all there isn't a lot of otter to aim at when all's said and done.

As he focused on the target, he was amazed to notice that what he had at first taken to be an otter was in fact a mermaid. Not just a mermaid, but a mermaid that appeared to be holding a child - hopefully she wasn't about to eat it. Showing a remarkable amount of restraint, he lowered his rifle, gently laid it on the ground and instead he took up his telescope, which - rumour had it - had been given to Colin in reward for his service on one of the ships that plied their trade upon one of the many seas.

Once again looking at the mermaid, this time with his vision improved by the telescope, he was able to make out more details. To his amazement he was able to confirm that she certainly had the upper body of a woman as he checked off the parts on his handy spotter's guide to mer-creatures:

- one head of fine hair: check,
- one head of human proportion: check,
- pink neck one: check,
- small rounded shoulders (well that rules out women Olympic swimmers): check,
- Finally, one set of breasts: and yep, on the list, it must make it a mermaid.

All that, but with the added bonus of her having a child held in her hands. During his many years at sea, and not to mention his time living amongst the Hebrideans on various of the islands, he had often heard tell tales of mermaids, but had never before been lucky enough to see one.

Being a man of deep faith, he offered up a prayer to the Virgin Mary for having stopped him blowing the happy little fishwoman to Kingdom Come. Whether it was that prayer, or the fact that he was a little clumsy with his telescope, the mermaid suddenly became aware of his presence. No doubt well aware of the danger involved in hanging around near a gun-toting crofter, and probably also well aware that a brick-carrying youth might be nearby, she and the child dived into the sea, never to be seen again by Colin Campbell. But that sighting was enough for him: until his dying day, he firmly believed that he had - indeed - been blessed enough to see a real, live mermaid.

Still not convinced mermaids exist, or at least *used* to exist, around these parts? Well how about one more tale? And again this one has a fair set of scales on it all the way down to the flipper.

For this report we head a little further south, and a little more towards the mainland, as we head to the Sound of Mull - a stretch of water that separates the isle of Mull from the Ardnamurchan peninsular. Once again, we are back in the distant - but not too distant - past as we join the South Uist crofter Neil MacEachain as he travelled back from selling his farm produce over on the mainland. As this was in the days before steam-driven boats had made it to the western coast, he had no choice but to take a sailing boat back home; quite an adventure, as even today the Oban ferry takes between 6 and 9 hours to make the journey, and that has a set of dirty, great, big engines to propel it on its way!

It's easy to imagine how unpleasant and demanding the journey would be; once past the shelter of the Sound of Mull the little boat would find itself out amongst the waves of the Atlantic, with still a long way to travel. As chance had it, the day that Neill was travelling was as calm as you would get, which would be great if you were on today's roll on/roll off ferry from Oban. I mean it would be a little dull, but the chances of sea-sickness would certainly decrease. However, in the days of sail, a very calm day would have a very different effect, and so it was that the little boat with Neill and his travelling companions, ended up becalmed. Still - at least - the sun was shining bright, and if they had been vain enough they could have worked upon their tans; after all, there was very little else to do except stare at the flat sea as it stretched towards the land on either side, and out to the horizon in front. However, sometimes when you aren't really expecting to find anything, the oddest things turn up, and in this case it was a mermaid.

As they watched over the side, they noticed close to the boat, maybe as little as only two yards away, a creature slowly emerge from the water.

Neill would later describe the creature as having the head, neck and breasts resembling those of a woman. However he would state that the hair was far coarser (I blame all that salt water) and that the eyes appeared to be glassier. The mermaid did not rise any further from the water than breast high so no detail of the lower half was gained. No doubt, all aboard were very glad that it wasn't blue and asking rhyming couplets. They just watched in amazement. For all his years travelling along the coast to and from South Uist to the markets on the mainland, Neill had never seen such a creature. Seemingly he wasn't the only one seeing something new, for the mermaid seemed equally amazed to see a boat full of men so close, as she just stared at them with large wondering eyes for a few minutes before silently sliding back below the water, and away from view.

While the majority of the men on the boat had never seen anything of its like before, there was one man who had, and he informed his fellows that they had indeed been lucky enough to have seen a real live mermaid. And how could he be such an expert on the subject? Well, simply he had seen one before some years earlier, while he was cutting kelp at Airdmaoilean back on South Uist.

Now it would be fair to say that those two tales are a little on the old side; a couple of hundred years old at least. And even the Babe of Benbecula is hardly fresh - having been lying in the ground for getting on for 140 years. But fear not! The tales of mermaids continue to within living memory, which considering that people reach a ripe old age in the Outer Hebrides, might not mean that recent. However, in the next case we are only talking just over sixty years.

Now, so far we have had sightings of the traditional mermaid from Barra, South Uist, Benbecula and Mull and hints of something blue swimming around the Shiant Isles in the dim and distant past. But for this report, we head off to one of the smaller isles in the chain. It's a lovely island even if it doesn't have the best of names. It is called Muck, and tales state that the island was referred to as the 'island of pigs' by seafarers eager not to use its real name, lest it bring bad luck on their vessel.

Despite its name, it is a nice little island; small but perfectly formed - around two miles wide, and only one mile long, giving a surface area of 1380 acres. Despite its size, it still supports a small population of around thirty people, and houses both a seal colony and a puffin colony on it shores. It lies just 10 miles north of the Ardnamurchan peninsula, well within mermaid-swimming distance of Neill MacEachain's encounter with one.

In 1947, an eighty-year-old fisherman on the isle of Muck came forward to report that he had seen a mermaid, and that she had been just twenty yards from the shore. He had watched her for a short while as she sat on a floating herring box that had been left in the sea, in which were preserved recently caught lobsters. The fisherman observed from the shore and was able to watch the mermaid undiscovered for a while, as she carried out that most traditional of mermaid activities: combing her hair, something that they seem to spend a lot of their time doing. (It's probably as a result of all that salt water that it needs to be combed so often). It didn't take long for the mermaid to become aware of the old man's presence, and as soon as she realised she was being observed, her hair-combing stopped, and she plunged into the sea, away from view. Like those before him, who had been lucky enough to see one of these rare creatures, he could not be shaken from his belief that he had indeed seen a mermaid.

So what are we to make of all these sightings? What or who are mermaids? A number of theories have been put forward over the years to explain the phenomenon, and the following are some of my favourites.

- They could be seals with their physical and behavioural characteristics being similar to those of a mermaid. The only problem is that if you live on one of these islands you are quite familiar with what a seal looks like. Even in the confines of Stornoway town it is not unusual to see a seal bobbing up and down in the harbour, and even the most tanked-up fisherman to fall out of the Clachan on a Saturday night has yet to be heard shouting 'It's a mermaid!' before falling base over apex.

- Another possibility is that it could be an as yet unidentified species of seal. Now, what if the seal in question is of a type that is so far unclassified by science; perhaps one that could actually pass for a human if only at a distance?

- It could be a sea ape. It has been suggested that an ancient ape, the *Oreopithicus* (an animal living in the Miocene period 8-7 million years ago), could have evolved into an aquatic ape. This is largely based on the fossil record that has shown that the *Oreopithicus* lived in a swampy forest habitat. Perhaps it then subsisted on a diet of aquatic plants. However appealing this theory is, it *does* have its question marks; for example, if an ape were to evolve from a watery habitat, it would be more likely to develop webbed feet and hands, rather than a fish's tail, and such a hypothetical creature couldn't explain the seal-shaped animal. Of course, the majority of the sightings in the Western Isles feature mermaids that are only visible from the waist up, which leaves open the possibility that they are without fishy tails.

- Yet another theory is that they could be an expression of the myth of the fish-tailed gods and goddesses of antiquity. But while Stornoway may have many similarities to Lovecraft's Innsmouth, and even a vague hint of the Marsh look among some of it inhabitants, it's doubtful that there really are deep ones living deep in the Minch. Still, it could explain why the town motto is *Ph'nglui mglw'nafh Cthulhu R'lyeh wgah'nagl fhtagn.*

SEA SERPENTS AND MYSTERY WHALES

Run for the hills; it's a Sea Serpent

It seems that the year 1808 was a good one for the sighting of mystery sea creatures, the most famous of which would be the one discovered washed up on the rocky shore of Stronsa (modern day Stronsay), one of the Orkney islands in September of that year. The carcass understandably caused quite a stir: the serpentine form stretched a full 55 feet from the head to the tip of its tail, and sported a fine crest that ran the length of the beast. Last but not least, it possessed six legs. Or at least that's how one witness described the remains to a Mr. Petrie who had been instructed to draw sketches of the creature. Unfortunately by the time Petrie was able to get to the site, the remains had largely gone - having been destroyed by a storm that had blown up and which had resulted in the rotten remains coming apart.

As there is yet to be discovered a vertebrate that has as many legs as the Stronsa beast, finding out what it could have been became a matter of great import to many people. Eventually the report of the sighting

made its way to Patrick Neil (who was the then secretary of the Wernerian Natural History Society in Edinburgh). He would in turn pass this information onto the members of the society at their meeting of 19th November 1808, when he told them of "a great sea-snake, lately cast up in Orkney". But the Stronsa sea serpent was not the only one Mr. Neil had heard about that year. There had also been rumours of one having been sighted in the Hebrides, not only by several fishermen but by a clergyman going by the name of Maclean. Could it be that the sea serpent that had been seen swimming about the Hebrides, and the one that had washed up on the shore of Stronsa were one and the same? Mr. Neil decided that he was going to find out, and set about sending letters out in all directions trying to locate any of the witnesses to that Hebridean sighting. His persistence paid off when he received a letter back from the Reverend Donald Maclean who, it turned out, was the clergyman rumoured to have seen it.

Luckily the letter would be preserved for posterity when, in 1811, it was printed in *Memoirs of the Wernerian Natural History Society*.

'To the Secretary of the Wernerian Natural History Society
Eigg Island, 24 April 1809

Sir

Your letter of the first instant I received, and would have written in answer thereto sooner, had I not thought it desirable to examine others relative to the animal of which you wish me to give a particular account.

According to my best recollection, I saw it in June 1808 not on the coast of Eigg, but on that of Coll. Rowing along the coast, I observed, at about the distance of half a mile, an object to windward, which gradually excited astonishment.

At first view, it appeared like a small rock. Knowing there was no rock in that situation, I fixed my eyes on it close. Then I saw it elevated considerably above the level of the sea, and after a slow movement, distinctly perceived one of its eyes.

Alarmed at the unusual appearance and magnitude of the animal, I steered so as to be at no great distance from the shore. When nearly in a line betwixt it and the shore, the monster directing its head (which still continued above the water) towards us, plunged violently under water. Certain that he was in chance of us; we plied hard to get ashore. Just as we leaped out on a rock, taking station as high as we conveniently could we saw it coming rapidly under water towards the stern of our boat. When within a few yards of the boat, finding the water shallow, it raised its monstrous head above water, and by a winding course got, with apparent difficulty, clear of the creek where our boat lay, and where the monster seemed in danger of being imbayed. It continued to move off, with its head above water, and with the wind, for about half a mile, before we lost sight of it.

Its head was rather broad, of a form somewhat oval. Its neck somewhat smaller. Its shoulders, if I can so term them, considerably broader, and thence it tapered towards the tail, which last it kept pretty low in the water, so that a view of it could not be taken so distinctly as I wished. It had no fin that I could perceive, and seemed to me to move progressively by undulation up and down. Its length I believed to be from 70 to 80 feet; when nearest to me. It did not raise its head wholly above the water, so that the neck being underwater, I could perceive no shining filaments thereon, if it had any. Its progressive motion under water I took to be rapid, from the shortness of the time it took to come up to the boat. When the head was above water, its motion was not so quick; and when the head was most elevated it appeared evidently to take a view of distant objects.

About the time I saw it, it was seen about the isle of Canna. The crews of thirteen fishing boats, I am told, were so much terrified at its appearance, that they in body fled from it to the nearest creek for safety. On the passage from Rum to Canna, the crew of one boat saw it coming towards them, with the wind, and its head high above the water. One of the crew pronounced its head as large as a little boat, each of its eyes as large as a plate. The men were much terrified, but the monster offered them no molestation. - From those who saw it, I could get no interesting particulars additional to those above mentioned.

The dimensions given to the head and eye may be exaggerated. It is remarkable that the animal is so often coming in the neighbourhood of a boat, and is yet perfectly harmless. This confirms my supposition expressed above that the animal is sometimes very inquisitive.'

With no report of any legs, and being considerably longer that the Stronsa sea serpent, it would appear that the two animals were not connected in any way (other than living in water). The Stronsa beast would eventually be labelled as being the remains of a large shark; a very large shark - as it would be similar in size to a whale shark. But if the Stronsa creature was *just* the remains of a shark, what was the sea serpent seen off the islands of Coll and Canna? And were the ships' crews wise in heading for shore and high ground? To answer the first question, it appears that it was a *bona fide* sea serpent, and to answer the question as to whether it was dangerous - well, it is claimed that in 1962, off the coast of Florida four young men were consumed by just such a creature, (the story being recounted in Richard Freeman's rather excellent book *Dragons: More than a Myth,*) and who is to say that the crews of those thirteen fishing boats had not heard tales of serpents in these northern waters taking a fancy to a human snack.

The Scales of Probability

Sometimes the sea serpents didn't just scare the living daylights out of those at sea, and sit in the water watching their victims run for the hills. Occasionally one would head for the shore for another reason, to just scratch an itch, or at least that is how the sighting at Griais was reported.

Many of these tales of mystery animals in the nineteenth century had no trouble making it into the letters page of *The Times*. I wonder if it would be as easy to get a letter printed reporting a sighting of a sea serpent these days. Whatever the challenges of getting one published nowadays, back in 1893 the Scottish physician W.M. Russell had no problems. Then again, perhaps he had been trying for some time, because he had found out about the sighting forty years earlier in 1851, when he had been in conversation with a certain Mrs. MacIver at her home in Griais on the isle of Lewis.

While her sighting had happened some time before Mr. Russell's visit, there is no firm date given other than around 1851, but the details were still fresh in her mind. She described how on the day in question she had been looking out from her house, across the expanse of Broad Bay to the peninsular of Point. While normally there would be nothing more to see than the usual clutter of fishing boats, this day would be different. There near the shore she could see a great commotion caused by fish leaping out of the water as they tried to escape a great sea serpent that was pursuing them. If nothing else this sighting suggests what a sea serpent's diet mainly consists of (that is when they aren't eating sailors).

But the peaceful scene of one of nature's wonders would soon be shattered, for as if Highland tradition demanded it, the local men ran for their guns and proceeded to shoot at the monstrous beast. Mrs. MacIver was certain that the men had wounded the unfortunate creature, but I would have to differ with her on that point. Can you really imagine for one second that anything short of coastal artillery would even dent the hide of such a creature? The much maligned sea serpent headed for the reef of Sgeir Leathann where it proceeded to raise not only its head but some eight to ten feet of its body up onto the rocks where it appeared to scratch some itch, perhaps dislodging the odd bullet that might have become stuck between its scales. It rested upon the rocks for a short time, until it was once again interrupted by the pursuit of the emboldened gun-toting locals who perhaps hoped to finish off the animal. No doubt thinking 'bugger this' the sea serpent slid off the rocks, and set off for deeper water, and away from the pursuing boats, leaving not only a great wake behind it, but also some of its scales. When the men in pursuit arrived at the rocks, they found a number of large scales that they understood to be from the creature, and after collecting some of them they headed back for shore.

Some of the scales would make their way into the ownership of Mrs. MacIver who would in turn pass them on to W.M. Russell who would rather carelessly lose them sometime before 1893. Despite his careless ownership, he did at least describe them before they disappeared for good. The description he gave was that the scales were both the shape and size of scallop shells. Let's just hope that Mrs. MacIver wasn't pulling the wool over the tourist's eyes with a couple of cheap ashtrays.

Sailing in the Sound of Sleat

Skye is separated from mainland Scotland by a sheltered stretch of water going by the name of the Sound of Sleat. While today the biggest thing you are likely to see on its waters is the ferry travelling from Mallaig on the mainland to Armadale on Skye, that hasn't always been the case, for back in the year 1872 it played host to its very own sea serpent.

It's hardly surprising that with the large coastline and sea-going communities there have been plenty of reports of sea serpents in the Hebrides over the years. Usually the sighting is limited to only a few hours at most, and at a distance, but the sighting of 1872 was different. This sea serpent turned up two days running, and its actions were recorded by a number of people. The principle witnesses were a sailing party, and as luck would have it they managed to get their account printed in the London based publication the *Zoologist* in May 1873 - all of which means we have the following account to ponder.

'Appearance of an animal, believed to be that which is called the Norwegian Sea-Serpent, on the West Coast of Scotland, in August, 1872 by the Rev. John Macrea, Minister of Glenelg, Inverness-shire and the Rev. David Twopeny, Vicar of Stockbury, Kent.'

'On the 20th August 1872, we started from Glenelg in a small cutter, the 'Leda', for an excursion to Lochourn. Our party consisted besides ourselves, of two ladies, F. and K., a gentleman G.B. and a highland lad.'

The names of the other people in the 'Leda' have since come to light. In his book *In the Wake of Sea Serpents,* Bernard Heuvelmans gave the names of 'F'. and 'K'. as being the minister's daughters Misses Forbes and Katie Macrea who made themselves known by letters sent to A. C. Oudemans; 'G.B'. was identified as Gilbert Bogle, the grandson of the minister. Gilbert Bogle had a letter published in the *Newcastle Weekly Chronicle* of 31st December 1877 recounting the events. This just leaves the highland lad unidentified. However I've been able to track down mention of that lad in a witness statement in *Peat Fire Flame* by Alasdair Alpin MacGregor, who discovered the name while interviewing John MacRae in 1932. John MacRae had been a boy at the time of the sighting living on Oransay on the Sound of Sleat and he identified the highland boy as Donald MacCrimmon who was on the boat to attend to the sails. Now that we have our full list of characters, back to the tale:

'Our course lay down the Sound of Sleat, which on that side divides the isle of Skye from the mainland, the average breadth of the channel in that part being two miles. It was calm and sunshiny, not a breath of air, and the sea perfectly smooth. As we were getting the cutter along with oars we perceived a dark mass about two hundred yards astern of us, to the north. While we were looking at it with our glasses (we had three on board) another similar black lump rose to the left of the first, leaving an interval between; then an other and an other followed, all in regular order. We did not doubt its being one living creature: it moved slowly across our wake, and disappeared. Presently the first mass, which was evidently the head, reappeared, and was followed by the rising of the other black lumps, as again. When they rose, the head appeared first, if it had been down, and the lumps rose after it in regular order, beginning always with that next the head, and rising gently: but when they sank they sank all together rather abruptly, sometimes leaving the head visible.

It gave the impression of a creature crooking up its back to sun itself. There was no appearance of undulation; when the lumps sank, other lumps did not rise in the intervals between them. The greatest number we counted was seven, making eight with the head, as shown in sketch N₁ 1. The parts were separated from each other by intervals of about their own length, the head being rather smaller and flatter than the rest, and the nose being very slightly visible above the water; but we did not see the head raised above the surface either this or the next day, nor could we see the eye. We had no means of measuring the length with any accuracy; but taking the distance from one lump to the centre of the next to six feet, and it could scarcely be less, the whole length of the portion visible, including the intervals submerged, would be forty-five feet.

Presently, as we were watching the creature, it began to approach us rapidly, causing a great agitation in the sea. Nearly the whole of the body, if not all of it, had now disappeared, and the head advanced at a great rate in the midst of a shower of fine spray, which was evidently raised in some way by the quick movement of the animal, - it did not appear how, - and not by spouting. F. was alarmed and retreated to the cabin, crying out that the creature was coming down upon us.'

The Rev. David Twopeny would later state that Miss Forbes Macrea was 'frightened out of her wits' so much so that she insisted on being landed at half past two in the morning, so that she could make her way home on dry land, walking the thirteen miles over the mountain tracks. She, of course, isn't the only person to decide that when faced by a sea serpent, the best place to be is well inland as far away as you can get from the sea.

'When within about a hundred yards of us it sank and moved away in the direction of Skye, just under the surface of the water, for we could trace its course by the waves it raised on the still sea to the distance of a mile or more. After this it continued at intervals to show itself, careering about at a distance, as long as we were in that part of the sound, the head and a small part only of the body being visible on the surface; but we did not again on that day see it so near or so well as at first. At one time F. and K and G.B. saw a fin sticking up at a little distance back from the head, but neither of us were then observing.'

Of those who saw the fin sticking up, Miss Katie Macrea described what she had seen: 'the row of lumps appeared again about a mile behind, this time a triangular fin stuck up from about the 4th lump and what appeared 10ft the size of our jib' while Gilbert Bogle commented: "I distinctly saw the colour of the creature and what appeared to be a small fin on the back or neck, moving rapidly sideways, and two or three yards behind the head. Its colour was a dark slaty brown, somewhat similar to that of a porpoise". There is, of course, no statement from Miss Forbes Macrea as she was hiding in the cabin at the time.

'On our return the next day we were again becalmed on the north side of the opening of Lochourn, where it is about three miles wide, the day warm and sunshiny as before. As we were dragging slowly along in the afternoon the creature again reappeared over towards the south side, at a greater distance than we saw it the first day. It now showed itself in three or four long lines, as shown in the sketch Nı 2, and looked considerably longer than it did the day before: as nearly as we could compute, it looked at least sixty feet in length. Soon it began careering about, showing but a small part of itself, as on the day before, and appeared to be going up Lochourn.

Later in the afternoon, when we were still becalmed in the mouth of Lochourn, and by using the oars had nearly reached the island of Sandaig, it came rushing past us about a hundred and fifty yards to the south, on its return from Lochourn. It went with great rapidity, its black head only being visible through the clear sea, followed by a long trail of agitated water. As it shot along, the noise of its rush through the water could be distinctly heard on board. There were no organs of motion to be seen, nor were there any showers of spray as on the day before, but nearly such commotion in the sea its quick passage might be expected to make. Its progress was equable and smooth, like that of a log towed rapidly.

For the rest of the day we worked our way home northwards through the Sound of Sleat, it was occasionally within sight of us until night fall, rushing about at a distance, as before, and showing only its head and a small part of its body on the surface. It seemed that on each day to keep about us, and as we were always then rowing, we were inclined to think it might perhaps be attracted by the measured sound of the oars. Its only exit in this direction to the north was by the narrow Strait of Kylerhea, dividing Skye from the mainland, and only a third of a mile wide, and we left our boat, wondering whether the strange creature had gone that way or turned back again to the south." –

'We have only to add to the narration of what we saw ourselves the following instances of its being seen by other people, of the correctness of which we have no doubt:

'The ferrymen on each side at Kylerhea saw it pass rapidly through on the evening of the 21st and heard the rush of the water; they were surprised, and thought it might be a shoal of porpoises, but could not comprehend their going so quickly.

Findlay Macrae, of Bundaloch, in the parish of Kintail, was at the mouth of Loch Hourn on the 21st, with other men in his boat, and saw the creature at about the distance of one hundred and fifty yards.

Two days after we saw it, Alexander Macmillan boat builder at Dornie, was fishing in a boat in the entrance of Lochduich half way between Druidag and Castledonan, when he saw the animal, near enough to hear the noise and see the ripple made in rushing along in the sea. He says that what seemed its head was followed by four or more lumps, or half rounds as he calls them, and that they sometimes rose and sometimes sank all together. He estimated its length at not less than between sixty and eighty feet. He saw it also on two subsequent days in Lochduich. On all these occasions his brother Farquhar was with him in the boat, and they were both much alarmed and pulled to the shore in great haste.'

Loch Duich lies two and a half miles further east, beyond the Strait of Kylerhea, and - once again - the fisherman's first reaction on seeing such a creature was to head for the shore. It makes you wonder if Miss Forbes Macrea knew what they knew when she decided to walk home.

'A lady at Duisdale, in Skye a place overlooking the part of the sound which is opposite the opening to Lochourn, said that she was looking out with a glass when she saw a strange object on the sea which appeared like eight seals in a row. This was just about the time that we saw it.

We were also informed that about the same time it was seen from the island of Eigg, between Eigg and the mainland, about twenty miles to the south west of the opening of Lochourn.'

We have not permission to mention the names in these two last instances.
John Macrae
David Twopeny'

There were a couple of other witnesses to the events. Bernard Heuvelmans provides the names of Lord Macdonald and his guests - including the Rev. McNeil, minister of Skye - who were aboard his steam yacht when they spotted the sea serpent in Loch Hourn on the 22nd and 23rd of August. Alasdair Alpin MacGregor adds another witness to the list, in the shape of John MacRae who as a boy, had seen the creature and would recall the events of that August sixty years later in 1932: "... [it] was as big and as round as a herring barrel, and of great length and it went wriggling up and down through the water, zigzag, right and left like".

The Reverend Twopeny added a little bit more to their letter in which he gives an account of another serpent sighting of Mull the year before.

'P.S. the writers of the above account scarcely expect the public to believe in the existence of the creature which they saw. Rather than that, they look for the disbelief and ridicule to which the subject always gives rise, partly on account of the animal having been pronounced to be a snake, without any sufficient evidence but principally because of the exaggerations and fables with which the whole subject is beset. Nevertheless they consider themselves bound to leave a record of what they saw, in order that naturalists may receive it as a piece of evidence, or not, according to what they think it worth. The animal will very probably turn up on these coasts again, and it will always be in that 'dead season', so convenient to editors of newspapers, for it is never seen but in the still warm days of summer or early autumn. There is considerable probability that it visited the same coasts before. In the summer of 1871 some large creature was seen for some time rushing about in Lochduich, but it did not show itself sufficiently for anyone to ascertain what it was. Also some years back a well-known gentleman of the west coast, now living, was crossing the Sound of Mull to the mainland, 'on a very calm afternoon, when', as he writes, 'our attention was attracted to a monster which had come to the surface not more than fifty yards to our boat. It rose without causing the slightest disturbance of the sea, or making the slightest noise, and floated for some time on the surface, but without exhibiting its head or tail, showing only the ridge of the back, which was not that of a whale, or any other sea-animal that I had ever seen. The back appeared sharp and ridge like, and in colour very dark, indeed black or almost so. It rested quietly for a few minutes and then dropped quietly down into the deep, without causing the slightest agitation. I should say that above forty feet of it, certainly not less, appeared on the surface.' It should be noticed that the inhabitants of that western coast are quite familiar with the appearance of whales, seals and porpoises, and when they see them, they recognize them at once. Whether the creature which pursued Mr. Maclean's boat off the Island of Coll in 1808, and of which there is an account in the Transactions of the Wernerian Society (Vol.I, p. 442); was one of these Norwegian animals, it is not easy to say. Survivors who knew Mr. Maclean say that he could quite be relied upon for the truth.'

The Reverend Donald Maclean's account can be found under 'Run for the hills; it's a Sea Serpent' at the start of this chapter.

'The public are not likely to believe in the creature till it is caught, and that does not seem likely to happen just yet, for a variety of reasons,- one reason being that it has, from all accounts given of it, the power of moving very rapidly. On the 20th, while we were becalmed in the mouth of Lochourn, a steam launch slowly passed us, and as we watched it, we reckoned its rate at five or six miles an hour. When the animal rushed past us on the next day at about the same distance, and when we were again becalmed nearly in the same place, we agreed that it went quite twice as fast as the steamer, and we thought that its rate could not be less then ten or twelve miles an hour. It might be shot but would probably sink. There are three accounts of its being shot at in Norway; in one instance it sank, and in the other two it pursued the boats, which were near the shore, but disappeared when it found itself getting into the shallow water.

It should be mentioned that when we saw this creature and made our sketches of it, we had never seen Pontoppidan's 'Natural History', or his prints of the Norwegian sea-serpent, which has a most striking resemblance to the first of our sketches. Considering the great body of reasonable Norwegian evidence, extending through a number of years, which remains after setting aside fables and exaggerations, it seems surprising that no naturalist of that country has ever applied himself to make out something about the animal. In the meantime, as the public will most probably be dubious about quickly giving credit to our account, the following explanations are open to them, all of which have been proposed to me, *viz:*-porpoises, lumps of sea-weed, empty harring [sic] barrels, bladders, logs of wood, waves of the sea, and inflated pig-skins; but all these theories present to our minds greater difficulties than the existence of the animal itself, we feel obliged to decline them

D Twopeny'

The Reverend Macrea also wrote an account to the *Inverness Courier* in August.

'Neither its appearance nor mode of progression had any resemblance to those of any known cetacean, shark or fish of any kind. In case any of your readers should imagine that I as well as the subject of my report am mere myth, you will please to give my name to this communication, and believe that among a pretty wide circle of persons who know me there is none who consider me capable of stating as true what I do not believe to be so; or so little acquainted with the sea, as not to know a whale, porpoise, a shark, or a herring barrel, when I see them.'

We can be in no doubt that both Reverend Macrea and Reverend Twopeny were quite certain in what they had seen, and were not going to be fobbed off with claims that the animal could not exist, and certainly were not going to believe it was just a number of random floating objects or a formation team of seals swimming in line. They rather favoured the mystery animal as being what they describe as a Norwegian Sea Serpent - so called because of the reputation of there being sea serpents living off the coast of Norway, terrorising the many fjords. These stories go back centuries; certainly as far back as 1555 when Olaus Magnus, the Archbishop of Upsala, wrote about such sea serpents, mentioning one 200 feet long that lived in the vicinity of Bergen. He filled his books with pictures of serpents generally attacking ships and eating the odd crew member. No wonder all those fishermen head for the hills when they see one of these creatures!

What Kätie saw

Right at the top of the isle of Lewis you will find the little port of Ness; the very same place from which the fearless guga hunters leave to hunt their dangerous adversaries. If you take the road to the village of Europie (Europaidh) and head past the restored twelfth-century church of St Moluag, you will eventually end up at the Butt of Lewis, in the shadow of the lighthouse that stands atop the towering cliffs. Sea birds fly around the rock stacks that are just off the headland. Behind the lighthouse, another mile down the coast, is the tidal rock stack Luchruban, which has acquired the name Pygmies Island because of the numerous small bones that have been found there, and all the time the Atlantic Ocean seems to be smashing against them. Beyond those rock stacks lies not a great deal, till you get to America; all right, you may hit Rona and Sula Sgeir, but if you manage to miss those lumps of rock it's America, next stop.

As you stand on top of the cliffs looking out across the dark water as it stretches all the way to the horizon, it is all too easy to imagine what mysteries lie beneath. But the chances are that even if you spent weeks camped up there with your binoculars trained upon the ocean, you might be lucky and see a whale. But it would be some going to see a real live sea serpent. Of course that isn't to say definitely that you *won't* see one, because on 7th February 1895, a Free Kirk minister going by the name of Berners claimed to have done just such a thing. He described a mystery sea serpent a mere 200 yards out to sea. The minister saw the neck of the creature rise about 15 feet clear of the water, describing it as resembling a giraffe neck, with something that looked like a ruffle two feet behind the ears. He goes on to describe that the animal had two great, staring eyes (that he likened to those of a bull), which were fixed upon him. How exactly he could make out this detail at such a distance is not, as far as I know, recorded. He goes on to describe what was visible of the beast's body; it consisted of three joints and was 120 feet long, each joint fitted in to the next like those of a lobster's tail.

The good minister's sighting is not the only one to have taken place off the Butt of Lewis, for only a few years earlier in 1882 there had been another sighting of a mystery sea creature. This one was spotted a little further out to sea than the 200 yards of the later report. This sighting actually took place eight miles west north west of the Butt of Lewis, and was made from the Stettin Lloyd Steamer *Kätie* as it was passing en route from New York to Newcastle. The Captain, Mr. Weisz, would report the sighting to the *Illustrirte Zeitung* newspaper as well as instructing the American animal painter Mr. Andrew Schultz to draw the creature. Of course if the sighting had happened these days, no doubt countless passengers would have recorded the whole thing upon their mobile phones, but as it is we will have to do with Captain Weisz's written account from the *Illustrirte Zeitung*.

'when the Stettin Lloyd steamer *Kätie* on her return from New York to Newcastle on 31st. of this year, shortly after sunset and in that clear light which the season prevails in the fine weather in the high northern latitudes, was about eight miles W.N.W of the Butt of Lewis (Hebrides), we observed on the starboard bow at a distance of about two miles, a dark object lying on the surface, which was only slightly moved by the waves; first we took it for a wreck, as the highest end resembled the bow and forepart of a ship, and the remaining hilly part resembled the broken waist-cloth of a ship filled with water. As we got nearer we saw with a glass on the left of the visible object, the water moving in a manner, as if the object extended there under the water, and this motion was of the same length as the part of the object visible above the surface.

Therefore we took care, not to steer too near, lest the crew should be damaged by some floating pieces of the wreck. But on getting nearer we observed that the object was not a wreck, and, if we had not known with certainty that on these coasts there are no shallows, we should have taken this dark connected row of hills for cliffs. When, however we changed our course obliquely from the object, which lay quite still all the time, to our astonishment there rose, about eighty feet from visible end, a fin about ten feet in height, which moved a few times, while the body gradually sank below the surface. In consequence of this the most elevated end rose, and could distinctly be made out as the tail of a fish kind of immense dimensions.

The length of visible part of this animal which had not the least resemblance to the back of a whale, measured according to our estimation, about 150 feet, the bumps, which were from three to four feet in height, and about six or seven feet distant from each other, were smaller on the tail end than on the head end, which withdrew from our observation.

At our arrival at Newcastle, I learned that some days before some fishermen of Lewis had observed the same or similar animal. Had I directly recognized the object before us, to be one of these creatures, which for so long time belonged to the fables, I should certainly have neared it with the *Kātie* as much as possible'

Despite the good captain mentioning that some of the fishermen of Lewis had also witnessed the creature, it appears that they left no written account of their sighting. Or perhaps they did, and such a report *still* awaits discovery. The great Bernard Heuvelmans - the father of cryptozoology himself - classed the mystery animal in this sighting as being an example of a 'many-humped sea-serpent', a creature that he proposed was to be found in the coastal waters of the North Atlantic, making the most of the warm waters of the Gulf Stream. He also noted that since the beginning of the twentieth century the sightings of this type of animal had become rarer.

You might be sorry if you catch it

Considering that Skye is separated from the mainland by only a narrow strip of water (the Sound of Sleat) it seems to have been host to more than its fair share of sea serpent sightings. In 1872, during the reign of Queen Victoria, the Reverends Macrea and Twopeny had had their encounter with a sea serpent towards the southern end of the Sound, while twenty-one years later all the action was to take place just beyond the far narrower north end in Loch Alsh.

The year was 1893, and a doctor from London going by the name of Farquhar Matheson, and his wife were happily sailing in Loch Alsh with the mainland on one side, and the isle of Skye on the other. You can imagine just how surprised they must have been, when - out of the blue - their jolly sailing trip was interrupted by a newcomer on the scene; the unmistakable form of a mystery sea creature. Dr Matheson would record the event as follows:

'Our sail was up and we were going gaily along, when suddenly I saw something rise out of the loch in front of us – a long, straight, neck like thing as tall as a mast. I could not think what it was at first. I fancied it might be something on land, and directed my attention to it. I said, 'do you see that?' my wife said she did and asked what it could be, and was rather scared.

It was then 200 yards away and was moving towards us. Then it began to draw its neck down, and I saw clearly that it was a large sea monster – of the saurian type, I should think. It was brown in colour, shining, and with a sort of ruffle at the junction of the head and neck. I can think of nothing to which to compare it with so well as the head and neck of the giraffe, only the neck was much longer and the head was not set upon the neck like that of a giraffe: that is it was not so much at right angles to it as a continuation of it in the same line. It moved its head from side to side, and I saw the reflection of the light from its wet skin.

I saw no body only a ripple of water where the line of the body should be. I should judge, however, that there must have been a large base of body to support such a neck. It was not a sea-serpent, but a much larger and substantial beast – something in the nature of a gigantic lizard. An eel could not lift its body like that, nor could a snake.'

Despite the obvious surprise at seeing such a mystery creature, the couple did not appear to be *that* fazed by their companion in the water, and they attempted to follow the creature as it swam off to the west towards the mouth of the loch, and out into more open water. They pursued it as best they could; observing that the mystery animal would in turn sink and reappear as it swam away. And swim away it did, leaving the doctor and his wife trailing behind. They can't half move these mysterious sea serpents when the feel like it, certainly faster that the average sailing vessel. A couple of things can be drawn from this sighting: once again it shows that your best chance of creeping up on a sea serpent was in the days of sail. It appears that the Victoria sea serpent would become scarce as soon as the noisier steam ships started to ply their trade. The other thing to note is the witnesses' reaction on seeing the sea serpent - not being local to the area, they proceeded to pursue the creature. Had they been locals, they would have been more likely to head for shore and run up the hills. It makes you wonder if they had managed to catch up with their long-necked saurian-type sea monster, whether they would have regretted their action: after all it might have been hungry.

I though I saw a sea serpent. Hold on, it's a...

It would appear that the golden age for sightings of sea serpents and marine monsters in the waters around the Western Isles was in the nineteenth century, when it seems you couldn't sail down the Sound of Sleat without bumping into one, and that just a little way off the point of Ness would have been a likely vantage point to spot something unusual floating on by. While today it appears that the great sea serpent is extinct in these waters, there was one last flourish of sightings in the early years of the twentieth century around the region to the south of the isle of Skye and stretching down to the small isles.

Three tales of sea serpents would be recorded by Gavin Maxwell in *Harpoon at a Venture*, a book that tells the story of his ill-fated attempt to set up a commercial shark fishing plant on the island of Soay. Despite his days fishing for basking shark, it would appear that Maxwell himself would not see any strange creature in those waters; however, his harpooner Tex Geddes would see something unusual in the waters around Soay in the late fifties. But that is an altogether different tale.

Going back a few years to the days when the basking shark factory was going at full steam, Gavin Maxwell came into contact with a couple of men who would regale him, and anyone else who would listen, with their own tales of how they themselves had seen a couple of serpents many years earlier. In an attempt to accurately record the details of those sightings that so often were told orally, he asked the two men involved to give him a written account of the sightings.

The first account is the sighting of a sea serpent made by Sandy Campbell. This happened while he was still a young boy, some time at the beginning of the twentieth century. Sadly, the exact year was not given, but the remaining details managed to be recorded in a letter that he wrote to Maxwell.

Sandy would tell the tale of how, when he was a boy, he saw a sea serpent in the waters between the isles of Skye and Soay. The sighting would take place on a calm autumn evening, when he had been among the crew of a small fishing boat that had set off to make the most of a bountiful harvest of herring. In those days, the seas still teemed with great shoals of them. It was not unusual on days like this for as many crofters as possible to head out into the waters in their little skiffs, attempting to make the most of the opportunity, and so it was as a result of this that the young Sandy found himself with two elderly men. One of them was his uncle, and the other a crofter going by the name of John Stewart. The three of them eventually found themselves in the vicinity of a small island at the head of Loch Scavaig. By this time they had separated from the main bulk of the fishing fleet, so while there were still plenty of boats out upon the loch that evening, they were now some distance apart.

By the time their nets were full, it was already dusk; the sky was still light, but the land about them was already dark, so with only a fine northern breeze to keep them company the three occupants of the boat started to haul their bulging nets aboard. Be in no doubt; it's hard work lifting heavy, fish-laden nets, and the two men, despite their advanced years, still had the advantage in strength and stamina over the young Sandy who was finding the hauling in of those nets particularly hard work, the lactic acid building up in the muscles of his arms. Stopping for a short break from the lifting, Sandy gazed out across the water to catch his breath, but what he observed as he did so fair took his breath away. For he noticed, barely 50 yards away, an object rising straight out of the water. At first it was only a yard or so tall, but as he watched in slack-jawed amazement, the object continued to rise until it was standing with a height in the region of 20 feet or more. As Sandy watched, he saw the tapering column moving to and fro in the air.

Understandably excited by the creature, Sandy tried to get the attention of the two men in the boat as they were still unaware of the sight in front of them, so busy were they trying to haul the nets aboard. They didn't at first take kindly to Sandy's shouting; it was bad enough that he wasn't helping with the load let alone the fact that he was making a racket. You can almost imagine the scene as old John Stewart looked up from the net, intent on telling Sandy to 'get his arse in gear and start hauling the nets aboard.'

The chances are that he never even got as far as 'to ge..' before he noticed what Sandy had been going on about. I bet the sight of a twenty foot object moving about in the air so close, was enough to make him think that a life ashore tending to sheep was a good idea. It didn't take long for the aura of shock to reach Sandy's uncle, who appeared to be the last man in the boat to see what was going on. All three of them stood and watched the spectacle in front of them. They could clearly see that this long neck appeared to be joined to a large dark mass that lay hidden for the most part below the water only occasionally breaking the surface. The sight left the three of them in no doubt it was the body of some animal.

As they watched, they saw the column start to descend slowly back into the sea in what Sandy would consider a direct reversal of his initial view. Once the great neck was submerged the animal started to move; which direction it took is not recorded, but what *was* recorded is that as it passed, the commotion was like that of a passing steamer. All of this was enough for the two old men in the boat to decide that they had had enough of fishing that day, and in a state of terror they abandoned the bulging nets, and headed for shore as fast as they could row (and it's surprising how fast old men can row, when they feel in danger of being eaten by a monster from the deep).

Once again the report emphasises that when local fishermen spot a strange undersea creature that suddenly heads in their direction, it is time to make for shore with great haste. Possibly this reaction is based on some local knowledge. Perhaps a variation of the Gallan Whale is in the back of every sailor's mind. Then again, it could have more to do with the seaworthiness of the small fishing boats of the time, and the danger of accidentally being swamped by a passing leviathan of the deep as it races off on its travels.

It seems that young Sandy wasn't the only person to have spotted something odd in the waters around Soay, because Gavin Maxwell also recorded another sighting of a strange creature; this time it was witnessed by two old men.

It was the following summer, that the two men had gone out to sea in a coble, fishing for lobster, and were rowing toward the island of Rum (later to be famed for its carnivorous deer). While the rowing might have been a little like hard work, at least the day was nice; the weather described as being not only fine but actually hot - a rare enough thing in these parts. But their peaceful day was soon to be ruined, as suddenly they noticed an object they estimated to be about 30 feet in height waving to and fro out of the calm sea before them. They thought they could clearly see a large body attached to that long neck, and worse still, that large mass was heading in their direction, and it was fair motoring. Once again the sighting was too much for the witnesses, and the two old men, scared out of their wits, decided 'bugger this for a game of dominos', and rowed as fast as they could for shore, and I bet on reaching the shore they didn't stop running till they had reached the top of the highest hill, as far away from the sea as possible.

In many ways the description points to the same animal as in the Sandy Campbell sighting, perhaps some kind of long-necked sea serpent was swimming around the area for several months. While the second sighting is said to have occurred the year after Campbell's autumn sighting, which would imply that the animal was in the area for nearly a year, I would suggest that possibly the second recorded sighting actually occurred before Campbell's, in the summer of the same year. Again the natural reaction was to head for shore. The type of animal seen fits neatly into the type of sea serpent that Bernard Heuvelmans calls the long-necked sea-serpent, a creature that is reported from around the world's oceans. It is suggested that this type of creature is certainly a top predator of the deep, most likely hunting fish, which in the early years of the twentieth century were still to be found in abundance in the waters around Skye. From other sightings of the long-necked sea-serpent around the world, it would appear that the type is capable of quite impressive speeds from 15, up to 35 knots. Such speed, and the long, flexible neck, would certainly give the animal an advantage in the catching of fish from the midst of a shoal.

There was one other reported sighting recorded by Gavin Maxwell, and unlike the first two, this report does have a year attributed to it: 1917. Given the year, it is unlikely that this sighting is connected to either of the first two (especially as by 1917 Sandy Campbell was serving in the Navy, and while the Royal Navy might have had some young lads serving in it, the chances are remote that Sandy Campbell was one of them). This time the report came from a Ronald Macdonald, and took place just off the coast of Skye.

The day of the sighting was a bright summer's day, and Ronald had taken his boat out to the mouth of Loch Brittle. While he was minding his own business, he suddenly became aware of something else sharing the water with him. He noticed an object around a mile seaward of his own boat. Ronald estimated that it was travelling at a speed approaching 5 knots. He would state that his mystery sighting appeared as a high column that he estimated to be a great deal higher than the neck of the beast that Sandy Campbell had seen over a decade before. Atop the long column, a light appeared to flash, Ronald would say of this that it appeared that a small head was being turned from side to side. While he could not see any portion of the body, he did comment that there was a considerable commotion in the water that lay astern of the long column. Eventually the column would slowly descend in a way that Ronald would describe as 'vertically, and without flexation', it would continue to submerge, until no trace of it could be seen above the waves.

While it appears superficially that this sighting is also of a long-necked sea serpent, it does seem to exhibit a couple of traits that to me suggest that it could be something quite different and possibly man-made. It is the behaviour of this 'mystery animal' that suggests a different cause. The first two accounts refer to the animal having a long neck that sways to and fro, whereas this mystery creature's neck is far stiffer; so much so that even when it submerges, it shows no sign of bending in any way, as it disappears vertically. This is something that more fits the theory that the object is metal rather than flesh and blood. In fact the only thing that implies any kind of movement is the flashing light that suggested the head was turning from left to right. It would seem odd that a flesh and blood sea serpent would have a head so reflective that the sun could bounce of it like a light when it was turned; that type of reflection is more often the result of a piece of glass catching the light, so unless this serpent was wearing a monocle it wouldn't really fit the bill.

Added to the stiffness and glass-like reflection from the head, there is also the description of the creature's propulsion through the water with a 'considerable commotion' appearing behind it, something that is not recorded from any of the other sightings, and despite that visible sign of effort the 'mystery animal' hardly seemed to be moving at a similar speed to its long-necked brethren just managing an estimated 5 knots, well short of the speeds that other sightings have produced.

When I put all those observations about this report together, I can't help but draw the conclusion that Mr. Ronald Macdonald had spotted a submarine in the act of diving; the long neck turning out to be nothing more than the periscope as it caught the sunlight on that bright summer's day. Never mind; spotting a submarine at sea must be quite a rare thing in itself. But if one sighting does turn out to have been a submarine, that still leaves two good sightings that suggest that the coast of Skye has played host to the long-necked sea serpent as it goes hunting.

Of what lurks in the Sound of Soay

A mile to the south of Skye lies the small, flat island of Soay. It measures a mere three miles by one mile, and is separated from Skye by a mile-wide stretch of water known as the Sound of Soay. Today Soay is largely deserted, the local community having been cleared in 1953 when all boats and services were removed from the island. But it wasn't always as deserted, and while it may be hard to believe today it was once the scene of an ambitious plan to turn the island into a centre for commercial shark fishing. This was the case shortly after the Second World War when a recently demobbed major going by the name of Gavin Maxwell bought the island.

Today, Gavin Maxwell is generally remembered as a conservationist, and author of *Ring of Bright Water,* amongst other books. It was one day in 1945 that he first happened to spot a basking shark swimming in the still waters near the island and it was this sighting that would lead to him setting up a commercial shark-fishing operation based on the island. He would end up building a shark processing plant. The main prize was the basking shark's liver, which contained the most valuable part of the fish; the oil, but the rest of the carcass also had its uses. Some of the flesh would be sold as food, some of it would be destined to end up as fertiliser, and the odd bit found life as an aphrodisiac, not like any of that would be of any interest or consolation to the dead shark. The shark-hunting operation lasted for just three years before the money ran out, and the gear had to be sold. Even so, during those few years it is estimated that a thousand sharks ended up being caught and processed. The shark-hunting consisted of harpooning the fish, and it was Gavin Maxwell's harpoonist Tex Geddes who is at the centre of the giant turtle story.

Joseph 'Tex' Geddes was certainly an interesting fellow, born in Peterhead in Aberdeenshire in 1919 and then, depending on which version of his life history you want to believe, he was either taken to Canada at the age of two, or less adventurously, he went to Easter Ross and was brought up by his aunt. Whatever happened in those early years, it is easier to know how he ended up harpooning basking sharks for Gavin Maxwell. It was during the Second World War; at a military training camp for Special Forces at Arisaig, on the west coast of the Scottish mainland, just across the Sound of Sleat from Skye; that the pair met. I have no idea if 1940s Special Forces training included using harpoons, but I suppose it could have been handy in hunting miniature submarines, which on the whole would have been similar in size to a full grown basking shark, and slightly more of a danger to shipping. So when Maxwell set up his shark-hunting business, who else did he choose but Tex Geddes to be the man with the pointy stick. It actually took a lot more than a pointy stick to stop a basking shark; the process would involve shooting a barbed harpoon into the creature then winching the fish to the side of the boat, where the *coup de grâce* was administered with a shotgun blast to the head.

As previously mentioned, the shark-fishing ended in failure, and the company being liquidated would in turn give Tex Geddes the opportunity to buy the island from the receiver - which is just what he did. While he was doing this, everyone else was getting evacuated from Soay. It was while he was the owner of Soay, that he would have his encounter with a mysterious giant of the deep.

It was on 13th September 1959 - six years after the evacuation - that Tex Geddes and an engineering inspector going by the name of James Gavin, who happened to be holidaying on the island of Soay, were privileged to encounter a giant turtle.

It was a fine day, the sea was calm and smooth with good visibility for a number of miles around, and Geddes was making the most of the conditions, intending to go out fishing for mackerel. It was while he was making his way to the boat, that he spotted James Gavin, a man he knew to be a keen fisherman, and asked him if he wanted to accompany him on the trip. Gavin was more than happy to

The basking shark fishing station was established here in Soay Harbour by Gavin Maxwell, on a small island off Skye. It operated between 1945 and 1948, when it collapsed financially, having caught around 1,000 sharks. The huge carcasses were pulled out of the water here, the livers rendered for oil, the rest sold for fertilizer, aphrodisiacs or food. A glorious failure of an enterprise. Ironically, considering Maxwell's reputation as a naturalist and conservationist, according to Hamish Haswell-Smith, (2004). *The Scottish Islands*. (Edinburgh: Canongate) This led to a serious drop in the numbers of these animals in the surrounding seas, from which they have yet to recover.

go with him. While out on the water, they had managed to spot some killer whales, and they even saw a basking shark, which must have breathed a sigh of relief that Tex Geddes had left his harpoon behind. Then James Gavin spotted something dark in the water around two miles away, in the direction of Skye, where they had earlier spotted the killer whales, but this object didn't strike Geddes as being one of these creatures. Its behaviour certainly did not resemble what he would have expected from a killer whale. For a start, there was no large fin sticking proudly out of the water; rather than a dorsal fin, it was the body of the creature that appeared to be standing high in the water - more like an overturned boat. But this was no boat, because as the pair eagerly watched, they noticed the animal regularly disappear below the waves, only to reappear a little later back on the surface, where it would be visible for a few minutes, before the whole process was repeated once more. Being a pair of observant fellows, the two men soon noticed that the mystery animal appeared to be heading directly for them. As it drew nearer, they could hear its breathing; a sound that Gavin would later liken to a loud whistling sound. It was both this noisy breathing, and the creature's steady movement towards them, that offered the first clue to the two men that whatever was heading their way was alive. This sea monster wasn't one of the high-speed Victorian types that so easily sent fishermen heading in a panic towards shore. Instead, it gently cruised along at a speed estimated to be no more than 3 to 4 knots. Nor did it possess the long neck so often attributed to sea serpents, but then this wasn't your normal serpentine mystery sea creature.

It didn't take long for the creature to be close enough to enable the two men to get a good view. Well, certainly it should have been near enough for a seafarer such as Geddes to identify it, if it had been something he had previously come across; but it seems in this case, it wasn't. For a start, it wasn't a basking shark, nor did it appear to be a whale. For as it got closer to them, they could see there were two distinct objects directly in line; the rear one appearing to be much the larger of the two. The two men stood frozen in amazement, as the creature slowly neared them. It appeared that some prehistoric monster was putting in an appearance just for them - lucky sods - for there, coming towards them, was a large reptilian head which Geddes would later describe as being in the region of two foot six high, with a pair of large bulging eyes. Gavin's description was in slightly easier-to-imagine terms, comparing the head to that of a tortoise, but being the size of a donkey, with eyes large and round, like those of a cow. Tex Geddes noted a large mouth, describing it as a large red gash devoid of lips that seemed to cut the head in half, whereas Gavin got the distinct impression of there being a set of large rubbery lips. When the mouth was open, he was able to see a number of tendril-like growths hanging down from the palate. They both agreed that the head rested upon a cylindrical neck that appeared to be around 8 inches in diameter, and that rose around a foot from the water. Behind the head, separated by a couple of feet of clear water, rose the rest of the animal; its back rose sharply to a high point, that stood some three to four feet above the water. After the peak, the back sloped down gradually towards the rear of the creature, some 8 to 10 feet away. The mystery animal would eventually get within 20 yards of the two men, who were still in a state of stunned surprise at the sighting. By the time it arrived at its nearest point, they were able to notice that the back seemed to be formed of a series of triangular spines - the largest of these being at the apex, with the rest descending in size, as they headed down the back to the water line at the rear. These spines did not appear to be mobile in any way, and were certainly not fins; it seemed that they were rather large, overlapping scales. The closer it got, the more apparent became the opening and shutting of the creature's mouth as it breathed.

Another thing upon which they both agreed was that the animal moved along with a very smooth, almost leisurely, motion as it progressed through the water. They both described in detail how it would arch its neck, and slowly the head would dive below the surface, and only when it was completely submerged would the large body follow suit and slowly slide below the waves. It would only take a few seconds longer for the head to break clear of the surface again to be followed by the large mass of the body; it seems proof enough to suggest the two objects were part of the same animal. On only one of the creature's dives did the two men notice any other supposed body part, a larger dark area well to the rear of the animal that they surmised was either a fin or foot.

They would be privileged to have a sighting for a full five minutes, before this mystery animal of the

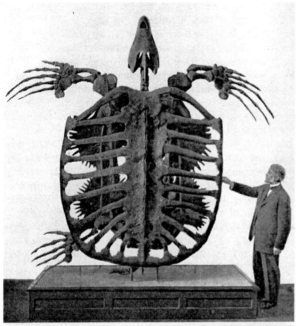

TOP: Archelon BOTTOM: Leatherback turtle

open seas dived below for the last time anywhere near them. Unlike the creature's previous dives, this one went on for much longer, and when it once again broke through the surface of the sea it was over a quarter of a mile away. Still in awe, the two men would carry on watching it as it slowly disappeared into the distance.

While Messrs Geddes and Gavin made the best report of the sighting, there are also rumours that the crews of two lobster boats fishing north of the little port of Mallaig may also have caught sight of this great leviathan as it serenely went about its business. Isn't it just a pity that mobile phones with cameras wouldn't be invented for a few more decades, or we could have had some wonderful pictures!

So what could their mystery creature have been? There are a number of clues in the description; the tortoise-like head, with its fleshy lips and a seeming absence of teeth in the mouth at the end of a long flexible neck, which in turn was attached to a large body that appeared to be covered in a hard shell. Certainly the features put together as shown in a sketch that appeared in the *Illustrated London News* strongly hint at it being a turtle of some kind, albeit a very large turtle. But do turtles really grow that large?

The largest turtle known to exist today is the leatherback sea turtle *(Dermochelys coriacea)* - one of which has been measured at 9 feet in length, which is quite a substantial size in itself. It might help if you imagine it as being about a foot higher that the average ceiling. But even a leatherback would appear to be on the small size compared to the remains of the largest turtle known to have existed, the *Archelon ischyros*. This turtle was to be found in the late Cretaceous period in the seas that once covered Kansas. The body itself had a carapace that measured 12 feet long, with a circumference of 25 feet, as well as a skull that measured a further 3 feet in length. While it might be of comparable size to the Soay creature, the carapace of the *Archelon* does seem to differ, in that it doesn't appear to have had the thick horny shell but rather the more rubbery type of shell of the leatherback. While the difference in shell makes a connection to the *Archelon* unlikely, it is hardly surprising considering the millions of years that have gone by since that prehistoric turtle lived. Rather, the *Archelon* shows that large turtles certainly did exist in the past, and perhaps some relation of it still roams the world oceans, and there *have* been sightings of some very large turtles over the last couple of centuries. In 1833 the schooner *Annie L. Hall* reported seeing a turtle that was described as being 45 feet long, off the Grand Bank, Newfoundland. There was another large turtle sighted by the crew of the steamer *Rhapsody* while steaming off Nova Scotia in 1956. They claimed the creature was 45 feet long, with flippers measuring in at 15 feet Compared to these two true giants the Soay turtle is a bit on the small side.

Of course the trouble with giant turtles is that they don't really have the pulling power of sea serpents or even the interest of a stray shark, as the great white shark flap of 2007 demonstrated. If an *Archelon* or one of its giant descendents were to be discovered living in one of the world's oceans, it is unlikely it would have the same impact as finding a prehistoric shark such as the *Carcharodon Megalodon* to be still swimming about in the ocean. After all, could you imagine the film *Jaws* having been so successful had it been about a giant turtle? But just because they don't have a media-friendly profile doesn't mean that they don't exist out there, hidden in the endless depths and open expanse of the world's seas.

If it smells like a globster, it could be ....

Over the years many things have washed up on the beaches of the Western Isles. Within the last four years these have included a couple of sperm whales that have not only become minor attractions, but also a source of an unbelievable smell. There is, after all, nothing like forty tonnes of rotting whale to clear the sinuses. They also attract a lot of seagulls for some reason. If the carcass fails to float out back to sea within a couple of days, thus removing the stinking remains to the deep, and far away from people, then the mortal remains will be put on the back of a low-loader, and dragged all the way to the council tip just outside Stornoway for burial, and quite possibly a chance to reacquaint itself with some of its new-found seagull pals.

Of course, sometimes the things that you find amongst the lines of rotting seaweed don't smell as bad. The empty beer bottles, and the pieces of wooden pallet that have escaped from somewhere, are not bad; just an eyesore. Whereas there are some things that have floated ashore, that are a bit more dangerous, such as the odd bit of military ordnance that has dropped off a plane, or fallen off a ship during one of the many military exercises that the islands get to witness on a regular basis. Every now and then, a relic of the World Wars makes an appearance, as a great, big metal lump washes up looking like a giant spiky beach ball. So it's best not to kick any of the strange lumps of metal that turn up, and better still, don't even think about hitting one with a hammer - you never know what might happen next.

Of course, not all the items that get washed up are so easily identified. Sometimes a strange lump of rotting creature will wash up on the shore, and these strange things go by the name of 'globsters'. It was the Scottish cryptozoologist Ivan Sanderson, who - in the 1960s - gave the name 'globster' to the random lumps of nondescript, putrescent carcasses that wash up on beaches all around the world. So rotten are these lumps of flesh and bone, that it's almost impossible to identify what they are actually the remains of. Perhaps they are the last remains of a sea serpent, but then again they could just be the last dregs of a shark that has seen better days, or maybe they are what finally happens to a dead whale that decides that it doesn't want to end up on the council tip. Of course, since the widespread use of DNA testing, it has become easier to identify what the globster started life as. Well, it would be if the results of the testing comes back as something that is actually on the database. Occasionally they don't.

With the widespread distribution of globsters, it would be unusual for one not to hit the coastline of the Western Isles, and one did just that in 1990. And where did it wash up? Benbecula, of course. Benbecula is an island whose beaches appear to be a magnet for all things mysterious to wash up on; from the body of a mermaid, to a 27-metre-tall metal silo that no one seems to want to own up to losing.

But it was neither a mermaid nor a silo that was the sensation of 1990. But being fair, the sensational find of 1990 wasn't all that sensational, until six years later when the picture of the globster of Benbecula unexpectedly surfaced in Northumbria.

Back in 1990 sixteen-year-old Louise Whitts was holidaying in the Hebrides when a journey down to the beach brought a surprise to everyone. There on the beach was their very own globster; a full twelve-foot-long lump of mystery whiffy flesh.

At one end it appeared to have the outline of a head, while along its back there were still traces of what appeared to be either the globster's gull- and fish-ravished flesh or its furry skin, but it was the fin-like projections that appeared to be along its back that drew attention. While the family might have wondered about what they had come across (perhaps they had found an unknown marine saurian from prehistory), there was one thing that they were certain about - and that was the smell. This was no fey globster. This was the real deal, with a smell so bad it could probably strip paint at forty paces. It was an obvious photo opportunity not to be missed, so a picture was taken of Louise sitting next to the beast. If one mystery is what the remains were, the other must be how she overcame the smell that *must* have emitted from the well-rotten carcass. Having worked in an office near to where a very large skate washed up, and had spent a couple of weeks rotting, I would recommend holding your nose.

Like many a holiday photo, the picture was destined to be forgotten and lost away at the back of a drawer. But unlike some long sought-after missing animal photos, it did make a reappearance in 1996 when Louise was moving out of her parents' home. Despite the intervening years, the creature in the picture was still a mystery, and curious to know what it was she had been sitting next to, Louise took the picture along to the Hancock Museum in Newcastle, with a hope that it could be identified. If only it was that easy to identify globsters. It wasn't unusual at the time for people to turn up at the museum with pictures of mystery animals, and up to that point they had been very good at identifying potential cryptids, but this time they were flummoxed. Never before had they come across an image of a creature so strange or as rotten as this photo opportunity. Their initial leaning was that the globster was possibly the remains of an unfortunate whale, but they couldn't be certain from the angle of the remains on the beach, and would bemoan the fact that they had neither more photos, nor - better still - the body, to poke about.

The picture went on public display that August, and the story made it into a number of newspapers. But despite all the publicity, the remains managed to avoid being firmly identified. Unfortunately, by that time, the chances of identification were extremely remote, as the carcass would have long since been washed back out to sea, or less romantically, just rotted away during the intervening six years.

A certain Cetacean

Given the location of the Western Isles it is hardly surprising that whales can be sighted from the shore, Whether it's killer whales in the Minch, or sperm whales off the Atlantic shoreline there are cetaceans to be seen; albeit most of the sightings of sperm whales in recent years on the isle of Lewis have come from strandings. As you may have already discovered, there are plenty of strange creatures that have been sighted off these shores, from lithe and seductive mermaids to giant sea serpents that once seemed to cruise the waters. But there are many types of mystery animal, and not all of those mystery sea creatures have to be as shockingly unknown as a forty-foot serpent, or a lass with a fishy tail. Sometimes the animal is of a type recognized by science, such as the whale. But, of course, just because whales in general are known it doesn't mean that all whales are known. If you consider that one whale going by the name of Longmans Beaked Whale (*Mesoplodon pacificus*) is only known from two skulls that have been recovered from beaches, and in the case of one of them it ended up on the floor of a fertiliser factory in Somalia, it is hardly surprising that more mystery whales are to be found out there in the world's oceans; after all, amongst that great expanse of water, it's easy to hide.

Amongst the first to record tales of mystery whales in these waters was the rather imaginatively named Martin Martin, or if you prefer the Gaelic Màrtainn MacGilleMàrtainn, whom we have met before, and who (as we have seen) in the late-seventeenth century, recorded various things of interest in the Western Isles. In his description of the isle of Lewis he tells of a particularly dangerous whale.

On the west side of Lewis can be found Gallan Head, a promontory that juts out separating West Loch Roag from the Atlantic. Out across the ocean, 21 miles from Gallan Head, lie the lonely Flannan Isles (the scene of the mysterious disappearance of three lighthouse keepers in December 1900), while inland from Gallan Head, is the village of Uig, and Loch Suainaval, once the home to a lake monster whose hunger was sated with the sacrifice of lambs thrown into the loch's deep waters. Of course, you would be looking in the wrong direction for whales if you were looking inland, as the whale sighting took place out to sea. Back when Martin was writing his travel guide, the waters around Gallan Head teamed with cod and ling. Understandably, such a bounty off the coast was not to be missed, and there would always be boats out fishing - a profitable but dangerous activity. Dangerous not least, because of the unpredictability of the sea, and also because it had been noted that around Loch Roag the whales tended to get in the way of the fishing boats. This was bad enough, but when you got as far as the waters off Gallan Head you had a particularly belligerent type of whale to deal with - the aptly named Gallan Whale.

The Gallan Whale was known for its great size, and it was only ever sighted off Gallan Head - hence its name. It was rumoured that the species occasionally produced man-eaters, as was the case in around 1680 when Martin recorded that such a whale was to be found in its favoured location.

A number of boats were out fishing for cod when a Gallan Whale appeared, and attacked one of the small fishing boats, destroying it in the process. Bad enough, you would think, being cast out into the waves by a grumpy whale, but imagine the horror - if you will - when the four fishermen realised that it was coming back to finish them off - which is exactly what happened next. The Gallan Whale returned to the scene of the wreck, and proceeded to eat three of the floundering fishermen before the eyes of the terrified crew of a nearby boat, as they desperately hauled the fourth fisherman aboard. He would survive the encounter along with the crew of that second boat, and they would provide the witness reports.

While whales might have been eating people four hundred years ago, it didn't take long for the roles to be reversed, and the hunting of whales would soon lead to their decline worldwide, and it would appear the end of the Gallan Whale, no doubt at the end of some exploding harpoon.

The next encounter with a mystery whale takes place around the year 1876 on the east side of Lewis in Loch Erisort and the balance of power has certainly shifted away from the whale.

On the day in question, a large shoal consisting of between 70 and 80 whales was sighted in the Minch, just off the entrance to Loch Erisort. It was assumed that they were chasing a large shoal of herring that had also been noted in the area. Seeing such a bounty so near to shore, it didn't take long to organise a few boats to go out and try and capture the whales. As far back as Martin in the seventeenth century the hunting of whales around Lewis had taken a certain form. He recorded that the natives, with as many boats as possible, would chase the whales into the bays, and then attempt to wound one of the animals and wait for it to beach itself, the hunters knowing that the rest of the school would follow that whale on to the shore where they could be easily butchered. Such practices could result in as many as fifty whales being run ashore, the whale meat being so plentiful as to be re-christened 'sea pork'.

So, obviously, the sight of so many whales swimming just off the entrance to a suitable sea loch was too good an opportunity to miss. Without a moment's delay, the boats set off and chased after the whales, doing their best to try and shepherd the cetaceans into Loch Erisort. Despite their best efforts, they only managed to force two of them into the confines of the loch - the remaining whales making a clean get-away into the depths of the Minch. The two whales may have been forced into the close confines of the shore side, but the boat crews were unable to drive either of them ashore. The tussle carried on for so long, that word of the two trapped whales made its way to Soval Lodge, where one of the occupants, a Captain Trotter, was a keen huntsman. So it was that Captain Trotter, his brother the Reverend Trotter, Miss Trotter and their gamekeeper Alexander Maclean, made their way down to the shore; the party weighed down with gun and spear. When they arrived at the scene, Captain Trotter made his way up to some high ground overlooking both the boats and the whales. I have no idea how good a shot the Captain was but I would imagine that a whale is a bigger target than a deer, so the odds were in his favour and with the advantage of the high ground, he aimed a shot at one of the whales, hitting it near the back fin. The shot didn't finish the whale off; that task was left to the gamekeeper, who proceeded to stride into the water up to a depth of five feet, before sticking the spear deep into the whale. The odds were certainly against the creature's survival, and so it would prove, but only after a further thirty minutes struggle after which its body was finally brought ashore.

Obviously, the second whale was having serious doubts about the wisdom of being as close to land as it was, and it made a new effort to escape the surrounding boats but Captain Trotter wasn't having any of that, (perhaps he fancied a whale's head trophy above the fireplace). He proceeded to shoot the second whale, disabling it and allowing it to be dragged ashore. So far it is just your usual tale of whale-hunting, but while the hunting may have been nothing out of the ordinary, the two whales were far from it. It was recorded that that particular species had never been seen on this part of the coast before; both whales described as being female with three fins - one on the back and two below, and with tail flukes described as being like a fan. The first whale measured nine feet with a head two and half feet long, and the second measured in at ten feet long with a circumference of seven feet. It was noted that there was scarcely any blubber on either animal. While the number of their teeth was not recorded, the size of them *was*; the length being given as about an inch, with the longest measuring one and half inches, all described as pure white and real ivory. Sadly, that is as far as the description goes - maybe a couple of true mystery whales, or just a couple of well known whales that no one recognised.

Of course, not all encounters with mystery whales start with a live animal; sometimes just the remains drift ashore. It isn't that unusual for the corpses of whales to get washed up. In the last three years (this was written in 2009) there have been reports of three dead sperm whales drifting ashore. If you are ever fortunate enough to make it to the west coast of Lewis, and to the village of Bragar, you will find the remains of another whale that drifted ashore. There, set upright as an arch in the village, is the jaw bone of a blue whale, and dangling from the structure is the harpoon that apparently killed it. I say 'apparently killed it', for when the dead whale washed ashore one autumn day in 1921, it had the harpoon sticking proudly out of its back. At a length of 85 feet, it was easy enough to identify this whale, but not all the whale remains that have washed ashore are so easily identified.

Such was the case in July 1961, when a badly damaged carcass was washed up at the far end of the Outer Hebrides chain, off the island of Barra. The remains, as they were exhibited, consisted of a long neck and a skull that was described as reptilian; but any excitement at the remains being those of a sea serpent, was soon dispelled when the zoologist Peter Usherwood confirmed that they were not the remains of a sea serpent, but rather a male beaked whale of uncertain species. If it had been a mystery reptile it would have made the front pages, but as it was just a hard-to-identify whale it was little more than a footnote.

LAKE MONSTERS

The inland sea serpent of Lewis

Well, you didn't think that the east of Lewis would miss out on its own sea serpents did you? After all, the west side has more than its fair share of large mystery sea creatures, and even the lochs in the centre are suspected to harbour the sea serpents' inland cousin, so what does the east coast have to offer?

Aside from the blue men of the Minch swimming around the Shiant Isles, it would appear at first; not too much. But that's before you have heard the tales of the serpents that turned up in the Leurbost area in the nineteenth century.

The village of Leurbost can be found in the Loch area of Lewis, an area known for its many sea lochs and small villages littering the coast between Stornoway and the isle of Harris. With the triple mixture of

land, water, and habitation, it's hardly surprising that at some time there would be a sighting of a mystery animal swimming up and down the lochs. Such a sighting occurred in 1856, and was reported first in *The Inverness Courier* and on 6th March 1856 it appeared in *The Times,* which by all accounts, makes it the first appearance of a lake monster from Scotland in the national press. The following account comes from the *Courier*:

'A Novelty in Natural History

'The village of Leurbost, Parish of Lochs, Lewis, is at present the scene of an unusual occurrence. This is no less than the appearance in one of the fresh water lakes of an animal which from its great size and dimensions has not a little puzzled our island naturalists. Some supposed him to be a description of the hitherto mythological water-kelpie an animal which figures largely in Highland Legend; while others, more dubious, and desirous to build their theories on historic fact, refer largely to the minute descriptions of the "Sea serpent *," which revived from time to time in the newspaper columns.

How these latter gentlemen propose to account for the reappearance of "His mightiness" in this remote quarter, we are not aware, but there can be no doubt that some animal or another, of an unusual size, is disturbing the waters of the lake in question. It has been repeatedly seen within the last fortnight by crowds of people, many of whom have come from the remotest parts of the parish to witness the uncommon spectacle. Exaggerated accounts are prevalent among those who have witnessed his evolutions, and are therefore to be received with caution.

The animal is described by some as being in appearance like a "huge peat sack," while others affirm that a "six-oared boat" could pass between the huge fins, which are occasionally visible. All however agree in describing its form as that of an eel; and we have heard one, whose evidence we can rely upon, state that in length he supposed it to be about forty feet. It is probable that it is no more than a conger eel after all - animals of this description have been caught in the highland lakes which have attained huge size.

Acting, however, on the supposition that the monster has a liking for the good things of life, the gentlemen renting the neighbouring shootings have prepared a floating apparatus, to which are attached several hooks baited with sheep, a cod, and a salmon, by which variety of delicacies it is fondly expected he will be induced to give a satisfactory account of himself. He is currently reported to have swallowed a blanket inadvertently left on the bank by a girl herding cattle, so it is hoped he will not be proof against substantial fare. Should the present means used for capture be ineffectual, it is intended to drain the loch, and thus secure the prize. A sportsman ensconced himself with a rifle in the vicinity of the loch during a whole day, hoping to get a shot, but did no execution.'

* The sea serpent in question is one that had gained a fair bit of fame a number of years earlier following the report in *The Times* of the sighting of a sea serpent by Captain Peter M'Quhae of the 19-gun HMS *Daedalus*. His letter to *The Times* gave details of how the ship had been passed by a 60-foot-long sea serpent while on transit back to Plymouth from the East Indies.

Well, what can you say to that?

The Highland gentleman - always ready to blast seven shades out of any mystery creature he happened across. Well, at least this one wasn't a great auk. Despite the fire power on offer, and the rather tempting cold buffet that was being dangled into the loch by numerous people, it would appear that the serpent of Leurbost was having none of it, and kept out of the way, and it would appear that it was never captured. Following the publication of the article, *The Inverness Courier* received a letter from a gentleman from London who wished to tell the tale of what he had observed while hunting on the island in 1821. The contents of the letter were as follows:

'Sir,

I observe a statement copied from your journal relative to a monster which has been seen in one of the lochs in Lews [sic] Island. 'I beg to inform you that when shooting in that island in September 1821, with four gentlemen, we saw the same animal and probably in the same loch; and for several hours endeavoured to get an opportunity of shooting at the creature, but without success. We dined that evening with Mr. Mackenzie, at Stornoway, and mentioned what we had seen to him. Mr. Mackenzie expressed considerable surprise, but stated that the report was current in Lews [sic] Island when he first came there, that such an animal had been captured in that very lake, and that it resembled in appearance a huge Conger eel and it required one of the farm carts to convey it to Stornoway. The capture of this creature must have occurred seventy or eighty years ago.

I am, Sir your obedient servant, W.P.'

Once again we encounter the gun-toting gentleman. I guess in the days before computer games, you could only blast *real* creatures for entertainment. Now, of course, you can shoot all kinds of imaginary ones without the need for fresh air. But aside from showing the dangers that awaited any animal that wandered past, it also suggests that the serpentine lake monster was once quite common. Despite W.P.'s suggestion that his sighting happened in the same loch, there is no real reason to believe that has to be the case. After all, there is a clue in the name of the area - lochs - that suggests that there is more than one large body of water that could hide such a creature. There is also the tradition of an animal going by the name of the *seileach uisge*, the water brute, or so it was recorded by an earlier chronicler of mystery creatures in the Outer Hebrides, who was told that the name could not be translated directly into English from Gaelic, but that the term would roughly translate as a creature known for both its repulsiveness and ferocity; something at which it excelled. So it is rather sad to report that the name literally translates as 'water snail'; perhaps to *some* repulsive, but hardly ferocious. In fairness, the term could have been used to describe a nameless beast that lurked below the still waters. Whatever the meaning of the name, this *seileach uisge* was an eel-like creature that would lie below the surface of its chosen watery home, and wait for some poor unfortunate to step into the water, only to be sucked deep into the depths, as the *seileach uisge* opened it great maw, creating such an inrush of water, that it would suck the unfortunate victim in. Eventually this water brute is said to have left its loch, and headed off to sea - perhaps on its way to the Sargasso Sea (possibly to join up with others of its kind). Mind you, it might just have heard that some gun-toting hunters were on the way.

But importantly, these three accounts suggest that there is - or was - a mystery water animal that resembles a large eel; a fact that sets it apart from the sightings of the water horses, a far more stocky animal than seen elsewhere on the island. It seems that there were plenty of reasons to keep clear of the dark waters of the lonely lochs of Lewis.

WEREWOLVES

The Where wolf

I bet you think that 'where wolf' is a spelling mistake - hardly the name of a mystery animal, and you would be correct. This tale is not about a where wolf, but the more easily recognised creature - the werewolf. Not just any old wolf/man hybrid, but a ghostly one that haunts the Hebrides. The trouble with this particular were-creature is just exactly *where* did the events take place? But that's racing ahead a bit; after all, you haven't read the story yet.

This particular tale first surfaced in 1912, in a book entitled *Werewolves* by Elliot O'Donnell (1872-1965). In the chapter entitled 'British werewolves', he first gives an account of a Welsh ghostly werewolf sighted in Merionethshire in the year 1888. The sighting featured a professor from Oxford who, whilst fishing one day in a local lake, managed to hook a skull of a dog-like creature. Being a curious fellow, he took the skull home with him at the end of the day's fishing, only to leave it on the kitchen table while he popped out for the evening with some friends. While he was absent, his wife (who was left in the house alone with the skull), became aware of a shuffling noise outside, and upon investigation, noticed a half-human/half-wolf creature at the window, which spent the evening circling the house, before it was observed to run off towards the lake, and vanish beneath its waters. The following day the professor returned to the lake, skull in hand, and threw it back into the waters, and that seemingly puts an ending to that particular haunting.

While the Welsh werewolf may have set the scene, it was the following tale that first introduced the Hebridean werewolf to the world.

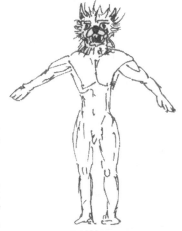

If we are all sitting comfortably, I shall begin to retell those events. According to Mr. O'Donnell, some years before he started to write his book on werewolves, he had uncovered *another* story of a sighting of a ghostly werewolf. This information had come to him from a source he considered to be the person in the story; a man whom O'Donnell would identify only as Mr. Warren. And if the identity of the man was a bit hazy, so was the location of the sighting. He only gave that as in the Hebrides, sadly a little vague on the whereabouts of the sighting, and - as you may already have gathered - the Hebrides do *indeed* cover quite a substantial area. But that is taking us away from the story.

The mysterious Mr. Warren recounted that while he was still a young lad, he had been living in the Hebrides with his grandfather, whose occupation was given as being an elder in the Kirk of Scotland (Church of Scotland). For the first few years he was living with his grandfather nothing particularly strange is reported, but all that was to change when Warren was aged fifteen.

As strange as it might sound, the young man's sighting was caused by the most mundane of hobbies. His grandfather was greatly interested in geology, and through a result of his hobby, he had started to fill the Manse with the many fossils that he had found in and around the many caves and pits that surrounded the area where the pair lived. It was not unusual for the old man to go out in the morning looking for more fossils to add to his ever-growing collection, but one day something unusual happened. The first young Warren knew of the strange events that were to unfold was when his grandfather came running back to the house in a state of excitement. So eager was the old man to show his grandson what he had found, that he was not going to take 'I'm not interested' as an answer, and soon the pair of them were out in the countryside, standing on the edge of a dried up tarn, looking intently into the bottom of it at the jumble of bones that lay exposed on the surface. You can almost imagine the old man's excitement, as he pointed out the remains to his

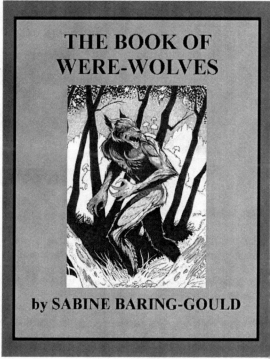

THE BOOK OF WERE-WOLVES

by SABINE BARING-GOULD

grandson. "Look, it's a human skeleton," he cried out. No doubt, looking a bit confused about the find, you can almost see Warren's blank expression as he looked on.

Unperturbed by his companion's lack of enthusiasm, the old man tried again: "What do you think it is?"

"A pile of bones; maybe some kind of monster," replied young Warren.

"Not just any monster; it's a werewolf," replied the old man triumphantly. I would like to think he was punching the air when he exclaimed it, but that might be asking a *little* too much of a Victorian elder of the Kirk.

Warren described how his grandfather then went on to tell him that in the past this particular island was known to have been overrun with not just werewolves, but satyrs. Once this brief explanation was out of the way, he urged Warren that they should take the remains home, so without further ado they gathered up the bones, and that all-important wolfy skull, and headed back to the Manse.

There are many remarkable things that happen in the final half of the tale, but the one I just can't get my head around is where they placed those bones. But I will let you make your mind up on that.

Once back in the Manse, they laid the bones out on the kitchen table (why, I ask you? Talk about keeping the kitchen clean). All day those bones lay on the table with no problem, but that evening things were about to change. It seems for some reason that young master Warren decided to stay at home that evening when the rest of the household set off for church. As this took place in the days long before computers, and the many games you can play on them, the young man sat down with a good book to read - perhaps glad of the peace and quiet that the evening brought.

It wasn't long before his reading was disturbed as he started to hear noises coming from the back of the house. No doubt carefully putting his book down, he set off into the kitchen to see where the noise was coming from. It soon became apparent to him that there was no-one about, and he thought that perhaps the noise had been made by rats scurrying about. Considering the cause of the disturbance to be as a result of rats, he promptly sat himself upon the edge of the kitchen table alongside the remains of the werewolf that, earlier that day, he had helped bring into the house. He sat there on the edge of the table, bored out of his tree, staring down at the floor; his legs swinging back and forth in a way that suggested a real level of boredom only to be found these day, in some of the dead-end jobs found in the civil service.

It didn't take long for his shoe-gazing to end, as he soon became aware of a rapping upon the kitchen window pane. Turning around to face the direction of the sound, he was startled to see a dark face staring back at him. At first it was hidden in shadow, but as Warren continued to look at it, the face started to get more solid, the details starting to fill out. While he *might* have been expecting the grizzled features of some ruffian to be staring back, it was an altogether more disturbing and possibly trouser-soiling visage that glared back at him; for there in front of him was a wolf's head that rather disturbingly terminated into the neck and shoulders of a man. It looked like the ghostly werewolf had come to collect its remains.

Getting his breath back from the initial shock, Warren began to study the features of the unearthly face that was snarling back at him. Looking around to see if the image was as a result of a reflection, he was soon able to confirm that this wasn't the case. There was no light coming from inside, and the only illumination from the outside was provided by the setting sun. With any optical illusion ruled out as a cause, Warren was convinced it truly was a wolf's head staring through the window. He noted the distended jaw, and the lips twisted into a savage snarl that displayed a full set of sharp white teeth. Aside from noticing that fearsome maw, he also noticed that the wolf possessed eyes of light green, and had pointed ears. Apart from the physical description, he also commented on the expression on that face - something that he would describe as being 'diabolically malignant', that appeared to be taking great delight in the young man's predicament. If anything, Warren's increasing terror seemed to encourage the beast outside. The werewolf raised one hand towards the window pane, and to Warren's undoubted surprise, this hand appeared to be slender and very much reminded him of the hand of a woman, albeit this woman's hand terminated in incredibly long and curved fingernails. Believing that this creature was not only evil, but intent on breaking in, Warren claimed that he crossed himself, but - to his dismay - it had no effect. Deciding that a good solid wooden door would be of greater use than faith, Warren ran out of the kitchen, slamming the door shut behind him, and ensuring it was firmly locked.

Later that evening the rest of the household would return from their evening at the Kirk. Upon telling his grandfather of the events that had unfolded earlier, the old man admonished his grandson. Obviously his failure to make the werewolf spirit depart was as a direct result of the young man's lack of faith, for of course the old man was in no doubt of his *own* belief. It certainly looked like the werewolf had given up by then, as there are no further details of it coming back that evening. Faith or not, the next morning Warren and his grandfather would gather up the bones and take them back out to where they had found them, and ensured that they were once again reburied, and by all accounts those bones still lie undisturbed.

While O'Donnell's first report of this sighting lacked both a full name for young master Warren as well as a firm location, all that had changed by 1991, when the details of the story were retold in the book *Scotland's Ghosts and Apparitions* by Terence Whitaker. The tale had gained a few extra details; Mr. Warren now had a Christian name, Andrew, and the location in the Hebrides had been fixed as being near Loch Longavat on the isle of Lewis. If that wasn't good enough, by the summer of 2008 you could find reports on the Internet stating that the werewolf skeleton had been found on an island on Loch Longavat. It all sounds very impressive, but even when I *first* read the story, I had a few doubts - especially when I read the account of the ghostly Merionethshire werewolf. It all seemed so similar that the stories could be twins separated at birth. It's not unusual to find certain local tales being very similar, you only have to look elsewhere in this book to see that the dragons of Islay and Mull shared a lot of similarities, so much so they could have crawled out of the same egg. Still, I thought it wouldn't be too difficult to find confirmation of the tale in other source material. Well, I have to admit that it proved to be a lot more difficult than I had at first imagined.

The first problem faced is the lack of a date. All that was stated was that it was some time before 1912. Assuming that Mr. Warren was not a centenarian, it would suggest that the events detailed must have happened some time after 1827, but I could find no tradition of werewolves on the island. Not a sign, not a sniff, not even a mucky paw print. The Hebrides might be up to their knees in tales of faery dogs and water horses; the waters around them might be chocker with sea serpents of every type, shape, and colour; but of a man with a wolf's head there is a definite lack of information. Still, I thought, Mr. Warren might only have confided in Elliot O'Donnell and no one else. After all, it might have been best not to shout about it, and worse it showed that he lacked faith, and at the very worst it suggested that he saw very strange things.

But just because the contemporary records appear to be lacking, it isn't really a problem as there are still plenty of clues that have turned up more recently; the location, for one. With the location originally being given as the Hebrides, it made pin-pointing an exact site difficult, but with the addition of 'near Loch Longavat on the isle of Lewis', things looked to be on much firmer ground. Of course, that was before I started to look at it in a little more detail. For a start, there *isn't* a Loch Longavat. There is, however, a Loch Langavat - well actually, there are quite a few of them in the Outer Hebrides; four, in fact. (This multiple naming is probably, in part, due to the fact that there was both a Norse and Gaelic tradition of naming places after prominent local features. Loch Langavat is not unique in this. There are, after all, five villages called Tarbert in the region). There's a small Loch Langavat on Benbecula - that small island with more than its fair share of creatures (but not a werewolf). Another one can be found in south Harris, a land renowned for its faery dogs (but they are all dog, not wolf). More promising are the last two Loch Langavats both of which are to be found on Lewis; there is a small one to be found on the moors north of Tolsta in the unoccupied land on the east coast - hardly likely to be the loch that we are looking for, after all it's in the middle of nowhere, and even the most optimistic estate agent would have trouble describing any property as being nearby. All of which leaves just one Loch Langavat to consider, and it's certainly the biggest of the contenders on offer. In fact, it's the biggest loch on the island, measuring half a mile wide at its widest, and a full seven miles long. You would think, then, that there would be plenty of opportunity for the house of an Elder of the Kirk to be built near its shores, but unfortunately, that isn't the case. While it might be the largest of the lochs, it is also one of the more remote, being devoid of habitation nearby, or even vaguely nearby.

Not being set back by the apparent lack of location, I tried to track down Mr. Andrew Warren himself with the aid of the online census. I was soon able to work out that there weren't that many of them about during the nineteenth century. In fact, I narrowed the search down to just the one individual who may have been the fellow who features in the tale, if in fact, the gentlemen's name truly *was* Andrew Warren. If the name is correct, it would appear that the sighting would have taken place roughly in 1872 (and I mean roughly) but even if the Andrew Warren in question *was* the correct one, there is nothing to connect him to the island, and this lack of detail added to the lack of a true location was really starting to get the warning bells ringing. Could the ghostly werewolf of Loch Langavat be a hoax?

While things were not looking good, there were still another couple of avenues to explore in the search. The next clue to the location was the nameless grandfather's fondness for collecting fossils from the location. Checking with a geologist friend, I was assured that the location was unlikely to be the isle of Lewis, due the island chain being made up of Lewisian Gneiss - a truly ancient rock around 3,000 million years old, which didn't leave much scope for fossils to be found in it (but what a revelation it would be, if anything were to be found within those rocks).

As you can well imagine, failure to confirm such important aspects of the report as people, place, and location was starting to suggest that all was not well with this particular werewolf story. But aspects of the tale *did* start to ring a number of bells. Was it possible that the tale had been embellished over the years from a number of different sources? According to information in Alasdair Alpin MacGregor's book *Peat Fire Flame* there was a case of ancient remains leading to a house being haunted. The story goes that in or around the year 1882 an ancient burial mound in the shape of a giant serpent was excavated at Scallasaig. A gentleman from London was responsible for the digging, and when the mound was opened, a big stone coffin was discovered, which was topped by a large stone slab. This slab was removed to reveal a large bowl reported to contain the ashes of a cremated person. Soon after being uncovered, the bowl was taken to the Manse (a house provided for a minister of the church, just such a one as Andrew Warren's grandfather) where it was kept for a few months before it was reportedly taken to a museum in Edinburgh. While the bowl was housed in the Manse, the building was haunted by strange noises. Could these noises be related to our missing werewolf?

Just when it was looking like the events might really have happened in the Hebrides after all, I discovered yet another version of the werewolf story. This time it was in deepest, darkest England. Christopher Marlow, author of *The Fen Country* in 1926, tells of the werewolf of Dogdyke Fen. A brief appraisal of the story reveals a number of startling facts that it appears to share with both the Loch Langavat and Merionethshire ghostly werewolf tales. Once again, our plucky young man comes across the remains of a wolf-headed skeleton. This time, the finder is a young archaeologist digging in the peat, and like the earlier protagonists, he takes his find home, and - rather tellingly - places the grubby bones on the kitchen table. Now if he had heard of the other two stories he wouldn't have been at all surprised when that night a ghostly werewolf appeared at the window. Again the lack of reflection is mentioned in the story, and once again, the young man's nerve fails him, and he runs off to another room, and promptly barricades the door, keeping the ghostly werewolf at bay. In the morning there is once again no trace of the creature, and as soon as possible he collects together all the bones and takes them back to where he found them and buries them once more. If nothing else, after reading this story, I am starting to suspect that the tale comes from some late Victorian horror story. Certainly the events described in the three tales failed to make it into Sabine Baring-Gould's *The Book of Werewolves*, published in 1865. In fact, in the book he goes on to mention the lack of werewolf tradition in Britain, blaming that on the lack of wolves in general in the country. Strange then, that within sixty years of Baring-Gould writing that, three stories of a werewolf should turn up. Still, I'm always one to give the benefit of the doubt, so I carried on looking into the background of the Loch Langavat story, to see what else could have crept into the re-telling of the story.

But there is something else that could have contaminated the report, and it comes from the big screen. Scotland has been the setting for a couple of werewolf films, the most recent being the 2002 film *Dog Soldiers* in which a small team of soldiers on exercise in the wooded wilds of the Scottish highlands have a somewhat bloody run-in with a family of werewolves that have been feeding on passing travellers. While the film is entertaining, the nearest it gets to being in the Hebrides is the Scottish accent of one of the soldiers; the film was actually shot on location in Luxembourg. While this film might be the latest to have a Scottish werewolf link, there is actually an earlier one, and not only is the werewolf Scottish, it is to be found living in the Hebrides. Could this have crept into later versions of the Andrew Warren tale?

Well, to assess if this is likely, we will have to consider *Dr Terror's House of Horrors*.

In 1965 the British horror film company Amicus presented *Dr Terror's House of Horrors* to the world; it would in time unleash a whole stream of similar compendium films - lots of little stories with twists followed by the really big twist at the end of the film. Once you've seen one, however, you pretty much know what's going to happen in the end. Anyway, back to Dr Terror and his house of horrors. The film concerns five gentlemen who happen to be sharing the same compartment on a train, when a little old German man pops in to join them. He announces his name as Dr Schreck, which he goes on to explain means 'terror' in German. It's not long before he manages to spill his pack of tarot cards on the floor of the compartment, and is enticed into telling the fortunes of his travelling companions. It is the first of these fellow travellers, architect Jamie Dawson, who is of interest in the search for the Hebridean werewolf.

After Jamie picks his first four cards from the pack, Dr Terror begins to interpret their meaning for the young architect, predicting that he will be heading back to his family home in the Hebrides to make some alterations for the new owner. While he is inspecting the cellar to the property, he uncovers an area of fresh plaster, and being curious, he removes it to reveal the empty coffin of Cosmo Valdamar, a wizard reputed to be a werewolf. It isn't long before staff in the house are being killed, and the countryside seems to be alive with the howling of wolves. Eventually Jamie attempts to shoot the werewolf with silver bullets he has produced from melted down silverware. Needless to say this doesn't work, and back in the carriage, Dr Terror reveals the last card as being death. When the shocked Jamie Dawson is asked where he is travelling to, he confirms that he is on his way to the old family home on the isle of Unga in the Hebrides, where he is to carry out alterations to the property for the new owner. Sadly, but not surprisingly, there in no isle of Unga in the Hebrides, but then it was only a film after all. So where does all this leave the search for the Hebridean werewolf that Elliot O'Donnell unleashed on the world in 1912? Well, certainly no further forward in digging up those bones that Andrew Warren sat next to on that kitchen table all those years ago. If anything, it appears to rule out Loch Langavat and the isle of Lewis as being the location, but that doesn't necessarily rule out the location as being one of the Inner Hebrides. And could it just be coincidence that the island of Ulva just off Mull was known to the Vikings as Wolf Island? Who knows?

So, at the end of that, am I any nearer to a location for this man-wolf? In a word, no. If anything, I am no surer whether the events happened in the Hebrides, Merionethshire, or even Lincolnshire. But at the present time I personally have my doubts that the events chronicled by Elliot O'Donnell happened anywhere, other than perhaps in the pages of a Victorian Penny Dreadful.

WATER HORSES

Each-uisge

What is an *each-uisge*? You may well ask. If I was to tell you that it was a 'water horse', would you be any the wiser? For those who have never heard of either, this chapter will hopefully be of some use to you.

One thing that all agree on, is that the *each-uisge* was a dangerous animal that lived in the freshwater lochs and rivers of the highlands and islands. Tradition is in no doubt that it was a dangerous creature to come across, that it feasted upon the flesh of man, and - depending on whose stories you read - it would either eat its victim's liver and leave the rest of the body to wash up on the shore of the loch, or it would feast upon the body and just leave the liver. It was *how* it hunted that takes it into the realms of the unbelievable, for it is said that the *each-uisge* was a shape-shifter, not the thing that your average mystery animal seems to have been big on doing.

When not changing shape the *each-uisge* would appear to be a horse-headed beast that lived in the dark still waters, and would - when hungry - travel onto the land where it would change from the ugly beast that it was in the water, to a fine horse that would appear to be tame and in need of a rider. If some poor unsuspecting person came across this horse, and decided that it was well worth climbing on, and riding it home, they would soon find out that it was a very bad idea. As soon as they sat upon it, the beast would suddenly become uncontrollable, and worse than that, the person would discover that they had become stuck to the creature. If that wasn't bad enough, it was probable that they would have heard tales of such creatures, and would know that only a watery grave awaited them. The animal would race recklessly back to its home in the loch, dragging the unfortunate victim - still stuck to its back - into the waters, where they would surely drown, before they would eventually - too late - spring free of the horse, enabling the *each-uisge* to eat whichever bit it wanted at its leisure. If nothing else, it tells you should never think about stealing a horse that has been left alone in a field.

Well, that's the generic version of tales concerning the *each-uisge,* but as the following examples show, each water horse appears to have very individual traits.

Our first tale brings us to the west coast of Lewis, and the tiny village of Shawbost. This shocking tale takes place in an area known as the 'Shieling of the One Night'. In a valley near to the village of Shawbost there was once a shieling. In case you are wondering, a shieling is a basic shelter; a small hut in which the drovers, shepherds and others who dwelt on the hills, would spend their time when the cows were herded up to the hills for the summer grazing.

This particular shieling had been built by two families who had agreed to share equal rights to it, which certainly aided the building, and helped with the upkeep of the hut. It was in the June following its construction, and at the beginning of the shieling time, that this particular hut had its first (and, as the tale

would have it, its last) occupants; they were a couple of cousins, both called Mary. Luckily for us, to prevent confusion, they were known to all by the names of 'Fair Mary' and 'Dark Mary'.

They had had a busy day looking after the cattle, and after milking their herd, they had both spent time at the churn, turning the milk. As the evening started to draw in, they found themselves sitting in the doorway of the hut spending their time knitting as they waited for the sun to sink away, awaiting the time for them to go to bed. In June, due to the northerly position of Lewis, it stays light well into the night, and if the cousins were intending to stay awake until it was dark, they would have a long wait ahead of them. Eventually it started to get dark, and one of the Mary's went to light the small iron oil lamp that hung inside the hut to provide a little light. Even as she lit the lamp, there appeared a woman walking towards their lonely shieling. Neither of the Marys had seen this woman before, but she appeared to be genuine enough, and there was no cause for concern, as everything about her demeanour and dress suggested that she wasn't anything other than a local woman. She introduced herself, and soon fell into conversation with the girls. She told them all about their surroundings - seemingly she knew everything there was to know about the glen and the neighbouring countryside; this quickly put the two cousins at ease, and when the newcomer explained just how tired she was after a long day's travelling, they offered her a place to spend the night, extending the traditional hospitality afforded to weary travellers in need of rest.

After enjoying a light meal, the three of them would soon retire for the evening. The interior of the shieling was a sparse affair, with nearly two thirds of it occupied by a very basic bed, which consisted of a mattress made from heather or straw that had been laid down within a rough wooden frame. Basic it may have been, but it was certainly comfortable enough for the three of them to soon fall asleep.

At dawn the next day, Dark Mary awoke and felt a warm wet patch at her side, she soon discovered that this was not as a result of an incontinent guest, for as she shook off her sleep she became aware that the mysterious guest had gone, and noticed with growing dread that the damp patch was a result of blood that had flowed from the breast of Fair Mary, who lay dead. Jumping from the bed, Dark Mary staggered to the basic door of the shieling in a state of shock. She flung the covering open, and gazed out on the glen, trying to spot any trace of the previous night's guest. Of the woman there was no sign, but instead Dark Mary noticed a horse trotting away into the morning mist. Upon seeing this animal, she was left in no doubt as to what had happened; she was certain that she, along with her cousin, had inadvertently invited an *each-uisge* in its human guise into their shieling. And that after it had killed Fair Mary, it had once again resumed its animal form, and was now heading off back towards its loch.

The body of Fair Mary would be buried on the slopes of the glen to the east of the shieling. After that fateful night, the shieling was never again occupied, and it would soon fall into ruin. From the events of that night, the area would get its new name, the Shieling of the One Night .

For our next encounter with the *each-uisge,* we travel forward from the time of murky myth and legend, into the age of reason, and the reign of Queen Victoria. The year is 1870, and around a small loch, Loch nan Dubhrachan, on the isle of Skye, a crowd is gathering - watching - as an attempt is made to catch the *each-uisge* that is reported to dwell within its depths. There are, of course, many semi-legendary stories of similar attempts to hunt a water horse by dragging a net through a loch, and equally as many different results, from catching nothing, to finding a very angry apparition appearing at the water's edge, and telling you in no uncertain terms where you can stick your net.

Loch nan Dubhrachan can be found on the southern most extremity of Skye, between the small islands of Ornsay and Knock; nearby is the Sound of Sleat, itself host to a number of mystery animals; but that is for another tale. This tale is different in the fact that it actually appears to have happened, and left plenty of witnesses to testify to the event.

For many years previous to the attempt to dredge the loch, there had been stories that the surrounding area was plagued by a creature that lived within the still waters, and which would travel abroad during the night-time in an attempt to waylay anyone foolish enough to get too close. But the *each-uisge* of this loch appeared to be more real than some of the others, and when it was sighted its description was far from being that of a woman in desperate need of a bed for the night. Rather, it was portrayed as looking like a dead cow. That is exactly how it was described during the one time that it was reported as being on the shore. The idea of it actually being a dead cow soon vanished from the observers' minds, when it moved from the shore and headed into the water. Once there, it proceeded to swim out into the deeper water all the time with its head below the water.

Eventually, the local laird Macdonald of Sleat decided that the time had come to see if there really was an *each-uisge* lurking in the waters of Loch nan Dubhrachan. The plan of action that he decided upon was to drag a large net through the loch, which would hopefully snare the beast.

Word soon got around the district, and when the day of the hunt arrived, there was to be found a large crowd surrounding the loch. They had come by cart, horse, and on foot. Local children had been let out of school, and the whole event was turning into a grand day out for all involved. The party atmosphere was no doubt helped by the liberal amounts of whisky that flowed around the crowd. It was said that there was more whisky flowing around than at a funeral, and it's a surprise, then, that anyone was still standing when the hour of the dredging finally arrived.

Those that were still sober enough to stand would have seen two boats, one at either side of the loch, with a long net stretched out between them; slowly the two craft made their way along the length of the loch. All was going well, until the net snagged on something. Had the *each-uisge* been captured? The gathered crowd certainly thought so, and a great deal of panic spread throughout them as they started to literally run for the hills, perhaps only then suddenly realising that catching a fearsome beast might be easy, but it doesn't make the creature any more friendly. Imagine cornering a tiger in your garden; at what point do you realise that it's bigger than you, and has lots of very sharp teeth?

Luckily for the fear-ravaged and quite possibly tipsy crowd, there was no fearsome aquatic man-eating horse in the net. Perhaps it had just snagged upon the branches of a sunken tree, or caught on a rock; either way it produced no creature. The dredging operation recommenced, and in time the boats would have reached the far end of the loch from where they had set out and all the laird would have to show for his troubles were a couple of pike that had ended up entrapped in the net. Still, looking upon the bright side, at least there are recipes for cooking pike, whereas not even Mrs. Beeton could help you with *each-uisge* although I would imagine if covered in batter it would go well with chips.

The next location that we travel to in search of the

each-uisge is the tiny isle of Eriskay, which lies two miles off the southern tip of South Uist. It's a tiny island, being just 2½ miles long, and 1½ miles across, at its widest point. Eriskay's main claim to fame is that it's the location of the shipwreck that inspired the film *Whisky Galore*, after the SS *Politician* ran aground at Rosinish Point one morning in February 1941. The ship contained just a mere 264,000 bottles of whisky alongside 90 crates of stout and the odd 60 cases of sherry, all on their way to Jamaica. The islanders retrieved an estimated 24,000 bottles of the whisky, before the authorities managed to put an end to their pilfering ways. Now it could well be imagined that with that much alcohol flowing through the veins of the locals, that there would have been plenty of sightings of water horses, and also that they could well have described any they saw as being big and pink with a trunk and large ears. But the sighting that we are going to look at happened many years before that date; it was in the year 1893 and there wasn't a shipwrecked bar in sight.

It was early one morning in June 1893 that Ewan MacMillan was wandering around in the mist that had enveloped the isle during the night. He was out that morning searching for his mare, which had managed to escape the day before, and it being a small island, he would have no doubt been certain that he would soon come across the horse. Eventually his searching would lead him towards Loch Duvat. It appeared that he was in luck, for there in front of him, shrouded in the mist, Ewan thought that he had indeed found his missing horse. As he walked towards the silhouette, there was surely no doubt in his mind. It wasn't until he got to within 20 yards of it; that he realized his mistake, the animal in front of him was most certainly not his missing nag.

Despite its diminutive size, Eriskay has many claims to fame, that have made the island well-known far beyond its local Hebridean region. It is associated with the traditional Hebridean song, the *Eriskay Love Lilt*; with the Eriskay pony and the Eriskay jersey (made without any seams).

Four years later, on the 5 June 1897 Ewan would tell Father Allan MacDonald, the parish priest for Eriskay and keen collector of Gaelic folklore, that due to the haze that June morning he had been unable to tell what colour the creature was, but he was confident in stating that the animal he had stumbled across appeared to be larger than the Eriskay ponies that are to be found on the island even today.

Almost as soon as Ewan realised that the creature wasn't his missing horse the mystery animal must have become aware of him, as it let out a terrifying scream that had poor old Ewan MacMillan running all the way home, no doubt for a change of pants. But he wasn't the only one who was unnerved by the noise, because the horses that had hitherto been grazing happily at the west end of the loch, also decided that they had urgent business elsewhere, and raced off away.

So there you have it: three very different examples of the *each-uisge* or water horse. What can we make of those tales? Well, for one thing it would appear that the *each-uisge* was not just a mythical animal that haunted the lonely places near the still, dark waters of some peat-infused loch, and that would, given the chance, pop out of the water, change into something else, lure an unsuspecting victim into its grasp, and pop back into the water and change once more into a horse. It would also seem that the term *each-uisge* was used to describe any large, mysterious animal that happened to pop unexpectedly out of a loch, or at the very least would run to hide in one if caught minding its own business on the shore. From the descriptions of the Loch nan Dubhrachan and Eriskay water horses, it would appear that if they were the same type of creature then the real *each-uisge* could be similar to the russet colour of the highlands. Without noticeable legs, could it be that these creatures were some sort of out of place walruses? But then again it sounds even more like a description of an errant Dougal from *The Magic Roundabout*. I wonder what his thoughts are about eating liver.

A paddock of water horses

It was remarked on by the prolific writer on all things Hebridean, Alasdair Alpin Macgregor in 1933, that 'belief in the existence of the *each-uisge*, or water horse, seems to have disappeared completely, it is only the matter of a few decades since every locality in the highlands and islands was reputed to possess a loch haunted by such a creature.' If MacGregor thought it was bad over 70 years ago that is nothing compared to belief today. It would be fair to say that mentioning a water horse today would just get you a blank look in return. It's a pity really, as I have happened across a fair number of tales, and it would seem a shame to hide them away unseen, so with that in mind, I think it is only fitting that these make the light of day once more. Now, no feeding the horses as we enter the paddock.

From the previous tales of the *each-usige*, it would be fair to say that they were right nasty beasts, and that you certainly wouldn't want to let one into your house and home. Just look at what happened to Fair Mary. But occasionally it would seem that you could meet one *without* ending up on the menu.

There once was an old widow who lived with her only daughter, in the west of Skye, in the area of Vaterstein. As fate would have it, the daughter was not a well woman, and in time she would succumb to some malady or other and spring off this mortal coil. The old widow's encounter with the *each-usige* would take place the night that her daughter died. She was alone in the old hovel of a house, the only light being produced by the glowing embers of the peat on the fire. Outside it was pitch black; certainly there was nothing that night that would seem to offer comfort to the widow, as she sat in that single room across from the cold corpse of her daughter. As she sat there mourning her loss that night, there came a strange man who wandered into the old lady's home. The widow had never before seen this man, but despite that, she allowed the stranger to sit down beside her, next to the fire, his hands resting upon his walking stick. As the evening wore on, the fire started to die down, but the stranger would soon get it roaring once more by striking the fire with his stick while saying 'O chaorain, dean solus!' which translates as 'O little peat, make a light.' Whatever was in his stick it certainly did the trick, and the fire would once again burst into life. The next morning when the widow awoke she found that the stranger had gone at first light, and she would not see him again. The people of Vaterstein were in no doubt that the old lady had been visited by an *each-uisge* that night in its human guise, and much against type it had appeared to have been there to offer comfort - it makes a nice change from eating the little old lady.

How do you follow the tale of a nice water horse? How about the tale of one being picked on by a feckless youth?

Once again we find ourselves on Skye, and another one of its lochans; this one could be found in the area around Uig. It was said that at the base of one of the mountain passes that are to be found in the area, there was a dark and brooding lochan, which in turn housed a dark and brooding water horse. Whether this particular *each-uisge* had a fondness for human flesh, or just liked sitting up keeping lonely widows company is not recorded, unfortunately; however, there was a sighting of this beast.

One day our feckless youth, a young herdsman, was wandering through the pass, perhaps looking for one of his herd (or then again perhaps he was just passing the time). Anyway, whatever his motive, he found himself on a precipice above the silent lochan. While peering over the edge, a mischievous thought entered his head; spying a number of large boulders nearby, he decided that it would be fun to push them over the edge of the precipice, and to watch them as they rolled down the mountainside towards the dark waters.

The trouble with large boulders is that they have a habit of being very heavy and difficult to budge. However, despite that problem, it didn't take him too long to find one that he was able to move, and with a little effort he managed to push it over the edge and watch with no small sense of satisfaction as it thundered down the hillside towards the water. On hitting the water, it threw up a tremendous splash, and sent waves rippling across the surface. The first stone was so much fun, that he decided to have another go. Once again he managed to find a large rock that he was able to push over the edge, and once again he watched as it plummeted into the water below. Again he saw the big splash, followed by the waves that rippled out from the point of entry. But *this* time he noticed that there appeared to be more waves and general disturbance of the water than the first stone had caused. As he looked down upon the scene, a little bemused at what was causing the commotion, he saw a mighty black steed start to emerge from the water. It took no more than a moment for the lad to realise that this could only be an *each-uisge*. Bearing in mind the creature's fearsome reputation, he dived for cover behind a nearby boulder at the edge of the precipice, and watched the unfolding scene while no doubt reflecting on his actions.

Down below at the edge of the lochan, the *each-uisge* rose completely out of the water coming to stand on the shore, and looking around for the intruder who had disturbed his watery home. Much to the relief of the young herdsman, the creature soon headed back into the dark waters, never to be seen again. But - then again - the herder never rolled any more boulders into the still waters of that lochan; after all, he might have been feckless, but he wasn't stupid.

So far, the *each-uisge* has behaved itself, and we can't let it continue like that; it's time that it reverted back to type, as the next tale from Skye will show (you might have noticed that the place seems to have swarmed with them in days gone by).

Once again, we find ourselves up in the summer shielings on the shadowy hill in the Trotternish. Once again, the tiresome but important job of looking after the cattle had fallen to the girls of the area, perhaps they always got the job to keep them away from the lads. But who knows? It could easily be just as likely that they were there to feed the *each-uisge*.

So it was one evening within their shieling hut, that two young ladies were settling down for the night on the large bed that occupied the centre of the room; the mattress consisting of layers of heather and bracken to make it comfortable to sleep on. Just as they were about to go to sleep, they heard a call from outside.

"Leigibh anstigh mi, a choloinn gaolach!" (Let me in, you beloved children).

The young lady nearest the door, got out of bed, and went to the door. Upon opening it, was faced by an old woman who asked her:

"C'aite an cadail cailleachag an nochd?" (Where will sleep the old woman tonight?).

"She will sleep at the feet of the maidens" answered the young woman, as she let the old woman in.

You would have thought that the old woman would have been happy with that, but the ungrateful old dear wasn't, replying: "Oh, but the beast of the feet will take hold of me!"

The ever helpful, if very naïve, young lady then suggested that she could sleep at the back of the maidens. Again, the old crone was unhappy at that suggestion.

"But what of the beast that haunts the back of the bed?" she asked.

That left just the centre of the bed to offer the old woman and that is what the young girl did. And so it was that the old woman made herself comfortable in the middle of the big bed, and soon all three were asleep. But as the night went on, the girl who had let the old woman in kept getting disturbed by her as she moved about the bed in a way that suggested to the girl that the old crone might not be a frail as she first appeared. It didn't take long before she felt that the old woman was crawling towards her, and by this time no doubt having her patience tested by this, turned to face the old woman no doubt planning to tell her to be still. If that is indeed what she had in mind, she never got a chance to say it, as when she turned, she was faced with something she wasn't expecting at all, the little old lady biting the arm of the other girl.

While she might not have been the brightest girl in the bothy, letting the suspicious old woman into the hut in the first place; she could tell an *each-uisge* when she saw one. There was only one thing to do when confronted with such a creature - the young woman started running. Luckily for her, she had a head start before the creature started to chase after her. At first it followed in the guise of the little old woman, but soon reverted to the more usual shape of the true water horse, shrieking loudly as it raced after the girl. Things were not looking too clever for our young lady, as she approached a little stream that ran between Totander and Balgowan, close to Bracadale church. Driven on by the pursuing *each-uisge*, the girl jumped over the flowing water, landing on the other side, just ahead of the water horse. Things really were not looking good for her, when a cock started to crow in nearby Balgowan. That crowing signalled the dawn, and had a magical effect on the water horse, making it unable to cross the flowing water of the stream, and thereby saving the young woman's life, and denying the water horse its breakfast. Thwarted as it was by this unforeseen event, the water horse cried out:

"Duilich e, duilich e, allian!" (Sad it is, sad it is, streamlet!)

So it is that the little stream came to be known by the name of Alltan Duilich, or the 'Difficult Stream'.

There you go; the water horse back to its usual behaviour, tricking its way into a shieling hut. Just *when* will these island girls learn that a strange weary traveller, knocking at the door in the night, could spell trouble? Of course, not everyone would fall for the trick. Occasionally they would notice that the weary traveller had something unusual in their hair; something that marked them out as a water horse, namely pieces of seaweed and sand.

Of course, there is another mystery beast in that story! 'The beast of the feet' mentioned by the old crone, and I am sad to say I am none the wiser as to what that could be.

Eventually, we come to our final tale of the water horse, and this one takes us away from Skye, out across the Little Minch, and then across North Uist to the Monach Isles, which lie just five miles west of North Uist. Today these islands are unoccupied, the last people leaving in the 1940s. These days they are just used as somewhere to put your sheep, and as an occasional stopping point for the odd fisherman. But it wasn't always the case. Once there were people who called these small islands home, and it was they who had trouble with a water horse.

The small village that was to be found on the island of Ceann Ear was close to Loch nan Buadh (the Loch of the Virtues). Unfortunately for the people of the village, this loch harboured a water horse that lurked within it depths. Even for a water horse it had a reputation for being a monster, far worse than any other water horse. It terrorised the locals, and they thought long and hard how they were going to rid the loch of this terrifying beast, but whatever they planned never seemed to work, and always ended in failure. Eventually things got to such a point, that the people of the village started to consider that there was

no option left to them but to leave the Monach Isles for good, leaving them to the evil creature.

But even as they made their plans for abandonment, a local woman by the name of Nicleoid came forth with an idea. She told the village folk that she had a plan to rid the island of the water horse for once and all. She explained to the crowd that she had for years been feeding and pampering a powerful bull which due to her lavish attention, had grown into a mighty beast, which she hoped would be more than a match for the water horse. As the village folk didn't really wish to abandon the isles, and could not see any harm coming from letting Nicleoid unleash her prize bull, they agreed to her plan.

So the day eventually came when Nicleoid led her bull down to the Loch of the Virtues for it to do battle with the *each-uisge*. Leaving her bull at the edge of the field near the water's edge, Nicleoid retreated to the far end of the field, to what she judged to be a safe distance from which to watch the upcoming battle. To start with the bull grazed happily, but it wasn't long before it started to get restive, tearing up the ground with both its horns and hoofs, and sending great sods of earth flying into the air as it worked itself into a frenzy, all the time roaring out a might-challenging bellow. It didn't take much time for the *each-uisge* to rise to this challenge, and it soon emerged from the waters of the loch, covered with weeds and mud from the loch bed. No sooner was it out of the water, than the fighting began. It appeared to those watching, that the bull had the upper hand - it being more use to being on land. But it didn't possess the fell cunning of the *each-uisge*, which started to back away, back into the loch. Sensing victory, the bull followed the *each-uisge* to the water's edge, and then - fatefully - into the waters of the loch itself, where it soon found that the water horse was much more at home than it had been on land. When battle was rejoined, it was anyone's guess which creature was going to come out of the contest victorious. As they fought in the water, a great cloud of spray was cast into the sky, hiding the two animal combatants from view. Only occasionally would the slightest glimpse of hoof or horn be sighted amongst the spray. As the village folk watched in amazement at the spectacle, it suddenly stopped, and the calm returned to the waters of the Loch of the Virtues.

Of a winner there was sight neither of the bull, nor of the *each-uisge*. The following day, a mutilated pair of lungs floated ashore, but they were so badly damaged it was impossible to tell from which of the animals they had come, but considering water horses' known lack of interest in eating offal, I would guess the late owner of the lungs was the bull. It is claimed that the marks left by Nicleoid's bull as it raked up the ground, can still be seen around the edge of the Loch of the Virtues.

It's not just a bull; it's a water bull

It would appear that at one time nearly every stretch of fresh water had an *each-uisge* lurking within its depth, waiting to trot out and lure the unwary to an unhealthy grave in either the murky depths of the loch, or perhaps in the digestive tract of the creature, offal aside, of course.

But not every creature of a mystical and perhaps not too solid a nature had such bad intentions in mind when they popped out of the lake. The small lochans and lonely tarns of the Western Isles occasionally harboured another water creature, the *tarbh-uisge* or the water bull. Unlike its horsy namesake, this animal was not seen as a danger, nor was it seen as often. Also, unlike the *each-uisge*, the *tarbh-uisge* stuck to the one shape - no turning into handsome men and wrinkled old crones for *this* animal. It was happy to stay in its true shape; that of a remarkably black bull-like animal. Certainly it appeared at a distance to be nothing more than a bull, but up close you would be able to notice that while it had the fine horns of a bull, it did lack any trace of ears. This lack of ears led to the belief that calves born with small or de formed ears, would be as a result of the union of a water bull and a cow; it seems the water bull had an eye for the cows.

As befitting a creature of such a shy and retiring nature, only a few sightings of it have been recorded, and all those that I have been able to find have come from the now largely deserted island of St Kilda. As the island was evacuated in the 1930s, it gives a clue to just how long ago these sightings were.

The oldest of those sightings happened so long ago that it was nothing more than a distant folk memory even to the last residents of the island. The story concerned the inhabitant of a seasonal lochan that was to be found only in winter time on the Mullach Sgar, St Kilda. With it being only a seasonal lochan, it does make you wonder where the water bull spent the summer, (not that it would really matter, as the tale only remembered the fact that one day a man passing by happened to spot the water bull near the water's edge, and in best St Kildan tradition, promptly shot it dead with a finely aimed arrow - there goes the first water bull to an all too common fate).

Now the next tale seems just a little bit odd, and the input of the water bull is at best limited, but bear with me - we will soon get to the animal in question. And it does seem to start off a little bit weird, but then who am I to judge such things? Anyway, it all goes something like this: one day, a woman on St Kilda was going about her business of carrying a big heavy basket of peats. She was carrying the load down a hollow behind the village, when - as if by magic - a tiny doorway opened up in the side of a nearby grassy mound. As startling as that event was, it didn't seem to faze the woman, who calmly put down her load, and hastily inserted her knife into the ground next to the door ensuring that it couldn't close. If it wasn't bad enough that a doorway to the faery kingdom had opened, it then spewed out a speckled cow that proceeded to drop a speckled calf at the startled woman's feet. In time the calf would grow up, and become a valued member of the herd, and there would be nothing to point to the animal's rather strange beginning. Eventually the cow in turn became pregnant, and the day came when its calf was delivered. All stood back in amazement, for the speckled calf had been born without ears. Okay other than the earless calf being its progeny, the water bull does seem to be absent from this story, but then again, tales of its amorous advances may not have been recorded for the sake of decency.

The final near sighting comes from Borerary, which is one of the islands that make up the St Kilda group. Upon this island stood an ancient structure going by the name of Stallar House; it was said to have gained its name from that of a man who had led a rebellion against the steward of St Kilda, but in fact, the structure would appear to be far older than the rebellion. Whatever its age, the structure was used for shelter by the hunters who travelled annually to the island on fowling excursions. On one of these fowling trips a number of men became stranded there longer than they had planned, as a result of inclement weather. Lacking a captive great auk to accuse of being a storm witch, the men's conversation soon turned to the subject of food, as they had not intended to be on the island that long and they were running short. As they sat around the fire one stormy evening, one of the men started to tell his colleagues of his desire for one of the Clan Ranald's fattest oxen (possibly in a sandwich, or maybe just a large Desperate Dan-style pie). No sooner had he mentioned his wish, than there was heard the lowing of a bull somewhere outside the doorway. While it seemed that the man's wish had been granted, they all knew that no such animal was to be found upon the island. Despite his wish for such a supper, the wisher was too scared to go out for the animal, and the rest of the gathered men were not much better, as they suddenly decided that they would rather stay indoors. It seems these men were not a patch on the peat-laden women of the main isle.

The next morning the mooing of the bull had long since

Samuel Johnson (often referred to as Dr Johnson) 1709-1784, was an English author. Beginning as a Grub Street journalist, he made lasting contributions to English literature as a poet, essayist, moralist, novelist, literary critic, biographer, editor and lexicographer. Johnson was a devout Anglican and political conservative, and has been described as "arguably the most distinguished man of letters in English history". He is also the subject of "the most famous single work of biographical art in the whole of literature": James Boswell's *Life of Samuel Johnson*.

ABOVE: Johnson BELOW: Boswell

ceased, and the men decided it was safe to pop out for a look. It didn't take them long to find a trace of the night's visitor; there upon the grassy slopes all around Stallar House were the prints of cloven hoofs. It seems that during the night they had been visited by a water bull; either that, or Old Nick had been sniffing about.

Boswell & Johnson and the water horse

In 1773, Samuel Johnson and James Boswell were touring the Hebrides, and as it happened, Boswell was making notes all the while, and would record the tale of a water horse that once inhabited a loch on the isle of Raasay - a water horse that had been a very naughty creature indeed.

Raasay can be found just off the coast of Skye, and can be reached via a short ferry ride across the Sound. Aside from the creature in the loch, the island already had a reputation as being the home of giants that had once ruled the Western Isles; that belief had led to the island being known as the 'isle of the big men'. It would appear, however, that they had long since departed before Johnson and Boswell made their trip there as part of their Hebridean tour.

When they finally arrived on the island, they found lodgings at Raasay House - the seat of Macleod of Raasay. By 1773 the island was finally recovering from the after-effects of the failed Jacobite rebellion of 1745, of which the Macleods of Raasay had been great supporters. However, following the defeat of the Clans at Culloden by the government forces, the Macleods paid heavily for their involvement, as those same troops would be sent to the island to lay waste to it and to put Raasay House to the torch. Despite all the government troops on the island, Bonnie Prince Charlie was actually able to find shelter there for a couple of nights, before heading back to Skye, and from there finding his way back to France and a gutter to drink himself into.

As it was, the house had been repaired by the time the two distinguished guests arrived, and it was none the worse for wear from its run-in with careless, match-tossing troops. Whether they saw any of the four ghosts that are said to haunt the building, is not recorded. Neither is it written down whether they saw the ghostly dog that is said to haunt the kitchen. If they failed to notice any spooks, they certainly did manage to be told about a fierce creature that had lived in Loch na Mna. Their guide recounted to them the tale of an animal, which Boswell described as being a sea-horse. While I couldn't say for sure, I don't think he meant one of those little critters that bob up and down in the water, and have a rather surprising reproductive process that sees the male seahorse getting pregnant. I rather suspect that the creature he had in mind was related to the *each-uisge* that seemed to haunt more than its fair share of lonely stretches of water, and had a fondness for eating people, and as far as I have been able to establish, did not have pregnant males.

Type of creature aside, the tale was roughly as follows: some time in the recent past, a local man had the misfortune to have witnessed his daughter being consumed by a wild beast that had erupted from the waters of the loch, and engulfed the poor girl. Understandably, the father was distraught at this unfortunate turn of events, and vowed to rid the loch of this monster once and for all.

He set about a plan to slay the beast. First he gathered up as many branches as he could, and made a pile of them a little way up the shore from the waters of the loch, all the time keeping an eye on the waters lest he become a target for the evil creature; after all, revenge is no good if you end up being the first course. At the opposite side of the pile of wood was a low stone wall, behind which the vengeful father intended to hide, awaiting the monster. Sticking out from the wall, he placed a great spit that stretched all the way into the pile of wood. With all the pieces in place, there was only one thing that the father needed for his plan, and that was a pig. Once the poor animal had been captured, it was slaughtered, and its still-warm carcass was tossed atop the pile of wood that the man then set alight, making a great fire that proceeded to roast the pig. As the smell of roast pork drifted to the loch side the man placed himself behind the low wall, keeping out of sight but with a firm grip on the end of the spit, and he waited for the beast to come. He didn't have long to wait. Out in the loch the water horse caught a whiff of the cooking meat, and started to make a beeline for the impromptu barbeque upon the shore. With a great splash of water falling from its body, the water horse stalked ashore and headed straight for the roasting animal. So intent was it on gaining the free meal that it was totally unaware of the man hidden behind the wall.

The water horse was soon tucking into the free food, unaware of the danger that it was in. It wasn't only the peril of eating undercooked pork that offered danger, there was also the red hot spit that lay amongst the glowing embers. But as it was, it didn't have time to really notice, as the grieving father took a firm grip of the spit, and drove the red hot tip into the throat of the beast, slaying it instantly.

By the time that Johnson and Boswell viewed the scene, all trace of the creature had long since gone, but the low wall that the grieving father had hidden behind was still there for the pair to observe.

But it wasn't the *each-uisge* of Loch na Mna that did for the Macleods of Raasay, it was another creature of the surf that occasionally puts in an appearance in the Hebrides; a mermaid. Or rather, a couple of mermaids. Well, to be more precise, it was a pair of statues of mermaids that the chief decided was just what Raasay House really needed. It was the chief's pursuit of these statues that would eventually lead to the family being bankrupted. After having the house rebuilt in the Georgian style in the nineteenth century, he had decided that what was needed was a pair of mermaid statues to go on the terrace at the front of the house. He couldn't find the statues locally, so he sent an artist off to Europe to track down a suitable pair. It was a good job for the artist as he was going to tour Europe at the chief's expense, but like all good things it eventually came to an end, and the artist returned with mermaids in tow. As it turned out they were two very big mermaids plus a rather sizable bill for the chief to pay. Being a tight fellow and on the verge of being broke, Chief Macleod refused to pay, stating that he has requested two life-size statutes of the mermaids and what he had received were far from life-size. Eventually the dispute went to court, and the court struggled to decide what that actually meant. In the end the Chief was financially ruined, and had to sell Raasay to an Edinburgh businessman, who promptly evicted the families living on the island, and replaced them with sheep.

If only the chief had popped across to Benbecula, he could have brought back the corpse of a mermaid, and won the case (mermaids aren't that big).

Make way for the 20th century water horse

Once upon a time, you wouldn't dare wander within half a mile of a lonely stretch of water without having to keep an eye out for strange ponies coming along with their big pleading eyes and comfy saddle; all too keen to offer you a ride into the dark waters, and have more than a nibble at you, liver exempted. Or maybe, while you were nervously looking at the still waters, a harmless little old lady would wander up to you, and inform you just how cold and far away from home she was, and before you knew it, having taken pity on her, she would be running amok in your house, having eaten another one of the occupants. Damned tricky things, these shape-changing *each-uisge*.

In his 1937 book *Peat Fire Flame*, Alasdair Alpin MacGregor would comment on the fact that by the 1930s belief in the *each-uisge* had all but died out throughout the Hebrides. It would seem that for some reason, people stopped believing in the creature, and the turn around in this state of affairs from belief to non-belief, had taken but a few decades. What had been the reason for this turn of events? Had the *each-uisge* become extinct?

You may have already noticed one thing about this mysterious animal that hides in the lonely lochs of the Western Isles. Up until the late-nineteenth century, the *each-uisge* was more of a fantasy animal than a real creature; more of a bogeyman that was used to tell children of the dangers of playing near water, in case they were to fall in and drown. No doubt, they were told to keep well away from the water's edge, or the *each-uisge* would get them. Similarly, from the tales, it would seem young girls were told of the dangers of strangers who they may come across in their daily lives, being reminded that even little old ladies could be dangerous, and perhaps were not to be trusted. To these 'animals of warning' no feat seemed impossible; after all it's hard to beat the ability to change shape at will.

But at the end of the nineteenth century, a new type of *each-uisge* was starting to appear: a more solid one, one so distinct that it would be better to call it by the English 'water horse'. This creature, unlike the *each-uisge*, appears to be a very real flesh and blood creature, for all intents and purposes a real mystery animal. In 1870 one was to be sighted at Loch nan Dubhrachan on Skye, leading to an attempt to drag the loch in an endeavour to capture the creature; and when Ewan MacMillan happened across a water horse while looking for his own lost horse in 1893, it was certainly a solid lump of mystery animal. However, when four years later he would report the sighting to Father Allan MacDonald, the priest would see the animal in the folklore tradition and would report it as such. It would seem, however, these last two sighting of the new, improved water horse would be the last in the Western Isles; a rather sad end to a new, more promising, animal. Or, at least, that is how it seemed for nearly seventy years - until a reappearance in the summer of 1961.

For most of the time the village of Achmore on the isle of Lewis has had just the one claim to fame: it is the only inland village on the island. In fact, you can't even *see* the sea from there. For me, there is another thing I always remember about the place: it was where I was chased by a dog while cycling (while Tarbert in Harris sticks in my mind as the place a chasing dog actually managed to sink its teeth into me). But aside from dodgy dogs and the inland location, Achmore would seem to have one more point of interest, even if it isn't all that well known. It was the place of the last reported sighting of a Hebridean water horse.

The actual sighting took place in a small stretch of water going by the name of Loch Urabhal. The loch in question can be found north of the village in the stretch of moorland that reaches up to the Pentland road, which runs from the outskirts of Stornoway, all the way across to the west side of the island.

So it was on the 27 July 1961, a bright and sunny day, that the sighting took place in a calm Loch Urabhal. The sighting occurred when two teachers, Ian McArthur and Roderick MacIver, were fishing at the shallow end of the loch. Whether they had any success in catching anything that day I couldn't say, but they did spot a rather big one that got away. No doubt peacefully fishing, making the most of the bright sun in the centre of nowhere, the two teachers were probably not expecting anything other than catching the odd fish to enliven the trip. That was until the point when Roderick MacIver jumped to his feet shouting: "there's something in the loch!" Much to their surprise, there was *indeed* something in the loch, and it wasn't the kind of thing you would expect to find. They would describe the animal as being around 45 yards away in the shallow end of the loch. As they watched, they saw it appear three times on the surface, giving them a view of a hump, and what could have been either a small head or a fin, some feet from the hump. They noted that the animal moved in a motion that reminded them of a dolphin; that is, it moved up and down in undulations. It may have *moved* like a dolphin, but it was much bigger, and considering Loch Urabhal is an inland freshwater loch, it's an unlikely place to find a dolphin anyway. Come to think of it, it's an unlikely place to find any large animal.

Whatever the creature was, it was certainly worth a picture, and Ian McArthur attempted to take one, but as in the best traditions of mystery animal photography, by the time he had prepared his camera, the animal had dived into the dark, still waters for the third - and as it turned out - final time.

Now, just because you have seen something, doesn't mean anyone is going to believe you. McArthur's father suggested to his son that there were no legends of a monster in that loch, and that they had probably just seen an otter. However, the younger McArthur pointed out that the animal in Loch Urabhal did not swim like an otter.

Dr Donald Macdonald, a Lewis historian, told a reporter for the *Glasgow Herald* that he had heard of no tradition of there being a monster in Loch Urabhal, before stating that the only loch in Lewis that was reputed to have a monster lurking in its depths, was Loch Suainbhal.

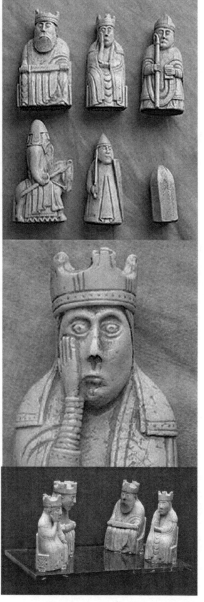

Loch Suainbhal can be found near Uig on the west side of Lewis. Uig itself is not famed for its nearby loch, but rather for a couple of other things. Firstly, the nearby sand dunes were the site of the discovery in 1831 of the twelfth-century Norse carved walrus chessmen, better known today as the Lewis Chessmen. Uig was also the birthplace of the Brahan Seer, a man blessed with second sight, and able to give startlingly accurate predictions of the future. He may have been blessed in one sense but he didn't seem too blessed with sense, as one of his predictions so annoyed the recipient, that he had him boiled to death.

While it might lack either Viking treasure or a famous son, Loch Suainbhal does have its own claim to fame. It is the deepest of all the lochs on Lewis, with depths in excess of 200ft. It was also once believed to have harboured its own lake monster, of which sadly not much appears to be known about these days, other than the fact that it was once deemed necessary to sacrifice lambs to feed the monster, lest it decide to pop out of the water and find its own food.

It wasn't the only sheep-eating monster to be found hiding in one of the many lochs that dot the island; there is also the tale of *another* creature that was to be found lurking in a lonely loch somewhere upon Barvas moor. It's difficult to know which loch the creature inhabited, as the tale is from long ago, and Barvas moor has the distinction of being one of the largest expanses of blanket bog to be found in the British Isles, and as such provides plenty of watery retreats for a devious water monster to hide in. But no matter how well the monsters may hide, they do have a habit of giving away their existence, for they have to eat, and their fondness for sheep is the problem.

So the tale goes that the crofters on the moor had started to noticed that more than the usual number of sheep were disappearing (sheep *do* have a tendency to disappear, even today, but that might have more to do with their ability to escape given the chance). Upon investigation, it was noticed that the sheep were disappearing in the vicinity of just the one loch. The crofters had their suspicions that there was something lurking under the still waters, and so they decided on a plan of action to find out what exactly in the loch was preying on their flocks. They certainly thought big, these crofters, as they decided to drain the loch; not an easy process, but they set about the task, digging a channel for the loch to drain through down to the sea. The trouble with draining lochs, is that it takes a fair bit of time for them to empty, and realising this, the crofters decided to head home for the night, leaving the loch to drain by itself.

Next morning, the crofters headed back out to the loch to see what the night's draining had uncovered. As it turned out, there wasn't much to find in the now drained loch; a few fish looking forlorn on the muddy floor, a bit of weed, but certainly no great big sheep-eating monster. That wasn't to say the crofters' efforts had been a total waste of time, because they could all easily see the slimy trail that led out from the loch down to the sea. It appears that their sheep-eating monster had taken the hint, and left the area for good, or maybe not ...for the odd sheep still does go missing.

FAERY COWS

There never seems to be an end to the faery animals that are to be found in the Western Isles. There are the faery cats - the *cait sith*; the faery dogs - the *cu sith*; and there are reports a plenty of faery folk living within any number of grassy mounds throughout the Hebrides. So it is hardly surprising amongst such things that there were also the faery cattle, the *crò sith*, to be found in various places.

Looking not dissimilar to normal cattle, there were still a couple of giveaways to their unearthly origin. For a start, faery cattle were slightly smaller than your normal highland cattle, and lacked any trace of horns. But the biggest giveaway to their faery origin, was that they had no problem swimming out to sea. Even more remarkable than that, they would live most of their lives under the sea and feed on the seaweed to be found on the seabed. The trait of living under the sea, and occasionally coming ashore to feed is in many ways similar to the equally mystical *sæneyti*, the Icelandic sea cow. However, there are a couple of differences between the two: the *sæneyti* was larger and possessed horns, and also featured a large air-filled sack on their nose, that allowed them to breathe under water.

Despite their preference for living under the sea, the *crò sith* occasional came ashore to graze; sometimes a faery herd keeper would keep a watchful eye on them; and they needed to, because given the chance, if a farmer spotted a faery cow on one of his fields, he would do his best to add it to his own herd.

One such tale of increasing the size of a herd in this way, comes from Harris many years ago, around the area of Luskentyre of the golden sands, and faery dog fame. One day, a herd of faery cows came ashore at Nisabost, and as soon as word got out of the animals being sighted ashore, the farmer and as many kinsmen as he could muster, headed off for the shore with whatever weapons they could gather together. They soon arrived down at the seashore, where they stood with the sea at their backs. They were a motley bunch; some - the wealthier ones - holding trusty swords tightly in hand, the poorer members of the group wielding wooden implements, and one poor sod just had a small twig in his hand. With arms stretched out wide, waving their implements, the group of men advanced upon the faery cows where they stood grazing. The intention was to drive the cattle further inland, and away from the sea, so cutting off their chances of escape. It didn't take long for the twig to break against one of the cattle, and it looked like the faery cows had found a weakness in the line, and would be able to stream back to the lapping waves and safety. In desperation, the former twig owner resorted in frustration to grabbing a handful of sand from the beach, and throwing it at the faery cows. Even as the first of them made it back into the sea, much to his surprise the sand did the trick; as the grains scattered over the cows, they turned away from the sea once more, and were driven inland. In the end, a good few faery cows managed to make it back under the sea, but even so, that night the farmer would have a new herd in the byre.

Of course, if the faery herdsman or herdswoman had been about, things *might* have turned out a little differently. The next herd of faery cows to consider came ashore on Skye near the rock of Macnicol on the farm at Scorribreac. Once again, word got around the area that the faery cows were to be found on the shore, and were there for the taking. So off the farmer and his kinsmen went to cut off the faery cattle from any escape back to the sea. Unlike the attempt to stop the faery cows in Luskentyre, there was no need for implements to corral these cattle. The tradition on Skye was somewhat different; all that you needed to do was to scatter earth on the strip of land that separated the cows from the sea. It was said that if the earth had been gathered from the burial ground, it would work all that much better in holding the faery cows back. With the help of a liberal scattering of earth upon the beach, the farmer had managed to capture the whole herd, and by evening he was able to sit back on his laurels and survey his new herd. But even as the farmer sat back relaxing, he started to hear an ethereal voice drifting in from the sea-shore. It was the voice of the faery herdswoman calling her cows home:

> 'Crooked one, dun one
> Little wing grizzled
> Black cow, white cow,
> Little bull, black headed
> My milch kine have come home
> O Dear! That the herdsman would come'

No sooner had the words reached the ears of the faery cows, than they started to make their way back to the shore. As their names were called, they soon broke through the little stockade that had held them back, and made their way towards the waves. Understandably, the farmer was having none of this. Having spent all day rounding them up, he wasn't just going to sit back and watch them run off back to the sea. So he ran down to the beach with great handfuls of earth to scatter in front of the herd. Scatter the earth he did in front of the approaching cattle, but to no effect. They just kept on heading towards the sea, trampling the farmer to death in the process. Eventually, all that was left to show of the faery cows' presence, were the tracks of their hoof prints leading across the beach, and into the sea, and the shattered body of the farmer lying where he had been trampled.

You see, faery cows might be gentle creatures, but the faeries were a pernicious bunch. So it wasn't wise to steal from them, for they didn't appreciate such thieving interference.

Scorribreac would not be the only location where the herdswoman was heard to sing to her bovine charges. In the *Camina Gadelica*, Dr Alexander Carmichael tells of a number of faery cows that came ashore at Obbe in South Harris, at a location going by the name of 'the Sruth'. It was observed that the faery herdswoman who accompanied the cows as they headed back to sea, sang to them a song the first verse of which was recorded, as she had sung it - rather surprisingly - in Gaelic. The English translation is as follows:

> 'A low is heard in the sea of Canna
> A cow from Tiree and a cow from Barra
> A cow from Islay, a cow from Arran
> And from green Kintyre of birches'

Luckily, it appears that no one attempted to get between the faery cows and the sea this time, as they headed back to their underwater home.

But it appears that not all faery cows lived out their lives under the sea. Others lived in even harder to reach places - as the final tale shows. On the small isle of Tiree towards the end of the eighteenth century, Dugald Campbell was tending the cows that belonged to the coastal farm of Baile-phuil. One day, while Dugald was out looking after them, he noticed that a new cow had joined the herd. This new red cow was smaller than the cows from Baile-phuil, and it appeared that the rest of the herd didn't take too well to the newcomer, and were soon setting about it with their horns. Fighting free from the onslaught, the small red cow ran off, not to the sea but inland. Even as it ran away, the rest of the cows followed in close pursuit, with Dugald running along behind trying to bring them back. As he ran, Dugald began to notice that there was something unnatural about the small red cow (for at one moment it appeared to be quite close, almost within reach, and the next moment it appeared to be as far away as it could possibly be). Could this red cow be a faery cow? It certainly looked like it had some strange powers. The pursuit carried on for a little while, but it wasn't going to continue for much longer, because the cow was heading straight towards the bare rocks of a cliff face. What happened next took Dugald completely by surprise, for as the little red cow reached the cliff, the rock face parted, and the faery cow passed inside, disappearing from view, before the rocks closed once more. Dugald looked on with a rising sense of dread as the Baile-phuil herd carried on towards the cliff face, before sliding to a halt just in time to avoid a painful collision with the cliff.

DRAGONS

The Wyrms of Islay

The island of Islay is the most southern of the Inner Hebrides, and a very long way from the storm lashed isle of Sula Sgeir far off at the north end of the Outer Hebrides. Islay actually lies closer to the Antrim coast of Northern Ireland, than to the Scottish mainland. Little wonder, then, that the Irish Celtic Scotti tribe that would one day give Scotland its name, would stop here for a few centuries, before heading off to conquer the rest of the country. And who can blame them? It's a lovely place to relax.

Today it's known mainly for having a name that is pronounced differently than how it's spelt (pronounced "eye-la", if you are interested) and for having more than its fair share of whisky distilleries; there being seven in total spread throughout the island.

Like the rest of the Western Isles, Islay was once occupied by the Vikings, and would from them become the domain of the Lord of the Isles, before coming into the realm of Scotland. Now, this tale takes us back to the time of the Vikings, and in particular, to a certain Goraidh Crobhan. Let's face it; that has to be the least Norse-like name you could come up with, but that was his name in Gaelic, and that is the language it was remembered by, and it translates as Godred of the White Hand.

Anyway, enough about the name - on with the tale. Old Goraidh was a mighty warrior, and had in 1066 accompanied Harald Hardrada, as that legendary Viking king attempted to take the throne of England, as Cnut had done fifty years before. But the best laid plans have a tendency to go a little askew, and in Harald's case, it was when he was met in battle at Stamford Bridge by the Anglo-Saxon army led by Harold II. At the end of the battle Hardrada was dead, and the Viking army destroyed. Despite all the carnage, (or maybe because of it), Goraidh was able to make good his escape, and head back to Islay and safety, well away from those nasty Anglo-Saxons.

Nevertheless, he was able to find yet more trouble in which to participate; not only would he go on to fight Fingal, King of Man, in battle, but then he would go on and have a go at Malcolm Canmore, King of Scotland. Eventually, Goraidh must have tired of all that fighting, and he settled down on Islay; maybe not the peaceful place it is today, but a lot more relaxed than the battles in which he seemed to usually find himself involved.

However, if he had expected a peaceful time, he was in for a shock, because during his absence Islay had been having a little trouble with a dragon. It had eaten most of the once plentiful cattle, and not satisfied with all those cows, it had also decimated the local sheep population, and had then taken a fancy to munching upon any person who happened to get too close to its lair at Imraconard. Plenty of warriors, both young and old, had challenged the beast, and the fact that their bones littered its lair showed that it was more than capable of looking after itself. It must have seemed to the dragon that all was going its way; that is until the day Goraidh Crobhan appeared offshore in his longboat.

Goraidh was dismayed to learn how the Dragon had ravaged the country and eaten his kinsmen, so at once he began to make his plans to rid the island of its presence.

On hearing tales of how those before him had gone to their deaths fighting the beast, he decided that such a fate wasn't for him; after all, he hadn't gone to the trouble of avoiding all those swords and spears in battle, to be eaten by a troublesome dragon.

The first thing he did was to gather as many barrels as he could, and tie them all together; he then placed them in position to lead from the shore to his ship where it sat out in Loch Indaal. For the next part of the plan, Goraidh had his crew hammer iron spikes into the top side of every one of the barrels until each one resembled a hedgehog full of sharp iron spikes. Once the spiky barrels were in place, he gathered together his three most flea-bitten horses for the next part of the plan. Setting off towards the dragon's lair with the horses, he travelled two miles, and then tied one of the nags to a tree. From there he rode on with the other two horses further along towards the lair. After another two miles, he again stopped, dismounted, and tied one of the horses to another handy tree. Mounting the final horse, he took his kite shield from his back, took a firm grip of his heavy spear, and set off once more towards the dragon's lair.

It didn't take long for him to arrive at the scene of so many crimes; as he scanned the area, his long hair was blown by the strong breeze that carried on it the stench of putrefied meat from the entrance to the lair. Goraidh could easily make out the remains of the poor unfortunates who had preceded him in their efforts to confront the beast.

It wasn't long before the dragon began to sniff out Goraidh's presence outside his lair, possibly alerted by the loud string of expletives that Goraidh shouted out trying to attract its attention. And get its attention he certainly did. The dragon came bounding out towards Goraidh. As it got closer, Goraidh cast his spear at it, only to see it bounce harmlessly off the dragon's heavily scaled upper hide.

The dragon lunged at the horse, but Goraidh had already wheeled the nag around, and was heading back down the hill towards his ship. Enraged that his dinner was heading away from him, the dragon set off after it, bounding along at a fair speed in pursuit. But if there's one thing we know about Goraidh, it's that he had a talent for escaping trouble; after all, he had managed to get away from the debacle of Stamford Bridge while the rest of the Norse army was slaughtered. And so with that experience, he was easily able to reach his next horse. No sooner had he reached it, than he leapt from the one he had ridden so furiously from the dragon's lair, and mounted and untied the horse from the tree, quickly releasing the rope, and setting off once more at a gallop towards his ship. He was just in time, as the dragon had finally caught up, but it stopped and leapt upon the poor, tired horse that Goraidh had left behind. The beast paused long enough to gorge on the horse, before setting off once more in furious pursuit. But however fast it moved, it wasn't quick enough to keep up with Goraidh - especially now that his new horse had seen what was in store for it, if it should slow enough to let the dragon get its claws into it.

Unfortunately for the horse, however keen it was to escape the fate of its predecessor, it soon started to run out of steam, and the dragon began to gain upon it. Just as it seemed that the dragon would soon get its large claws into Goraidh, the next horse came into sight, tied to its tree. Leaping from the back of the second horse, Goraidh landed upon the third one just as the dragon pounced on the previous mount. Once again, it was unable to resist having a nibble on the fresh kill, and started to eat the unfortunate mare. This delay gave Goraidh just enough time to free his horse, and set off once more towards his longboat that lay tied up out in the bay. It didn't take long for the dragon to finish off the horse, and once again it set off in pursuit of the fleeing man, but despite the poor state of the remaining horse, the dragon - having by this time eaten so much - was barely able to gain on it, despite being driven on to continue the chase by Goraidh's never-ending stream of insults, ('call yourself a dragon' and the like).

Soon, Goraidh arrived at the beach, where he leapt from the tired horse, and ran towards the barrel causeway that led out to his ship. No sooner had he started on the causeway, weaving in and out of the wickedly sharp iron spikes, than the dragon arrived on the beach, and instantly set about finishing off the last of the horses. By this time, no doubt tiring of horse meat and relishing the idea of a taste of human, it spied that Goraidh had run out of horses, and was unable to escape, having run onto his ship, and to what was most certainly a dead end.

Summoning all its animal cunning, the dragon launched itself towards the ship, and began running over the barrel causeway, but its journey was not as easy as that of Goraidh's. The low-lying belly of the dragon, distended as it was by all that horse meat, snagged upon the spikes, while no doubt frustration and anger propelled it ever onwards towards the laughing Goraidh. But with each step, as it tried to get closer, the dragon only succeeded in impaling itself further onto the iron spikes, until it had managed to skewer itself completely. Only when the dragon was completely immobile, and bleeding heavily from its many wounds, did Goraidh head towards it - his mighty war axe in hand. Upon reaching the prone beast, he raised his axe high above his head with both hands, before bringing the glistening blade down to sever the creature's head from its body. And so ended the dragon's reign of terror on Islay.

Now, you have to admit that that tale has more than a fair share of fantasy about it. Certainly it's not unusual for the local hero figure to slay the local dragon. Goraidh does better than most, as he seems to have survived his battle with the dragon without something unfortunate happening at the end such as snagging himself on a poisoned tooth or such like.

But perhaps, once upon a time, there really was something large and dragon-like that inhabited the island. So what should we make of the following tale? Could it hold a clue to the mystery of the Dragon of Islay?

Today you might be lucky enough to come across an adder basking in the sunshine up on one of the moors. Hardly a highly dangerous beast, although it certainly has a poisonous bite, but you would be rather unlucky if it were to bite you. And even if it *did*, the chances are that you would survive if you are in good health (but better not take my word for it as I'm no snake expert). An adder is hardly the kind of creature that would strike fear throughout the island, nor would it need a knight in shining armour to come and save the day with his cunning horse and barrel trick. After all, an adder is only a couple of feet long at best.

In the early years of the nineteenth century a snake was killed at Bailemonaidh on Islay. Nothing all that remarkable in the event itself, but what *is* remarkable are the measurements of the slain creature. It measured nine feet in length, and had a circumference of eighteen inches. It was hardly your common-or-garden adder. Its demise came as a result of its reported fondness for milk, of all things. So how did all this come about?

Well, one summer the occupants of one of the summer sheilings noticed that every morning the level of the contents of their milk barrel was lower than it had been the previous evening. Eventually the occupants tired of this nightly loss, and decided to track down the culprit. Luck was on their side. As they searched around the field, they happened to come across a trace of some spilt milk, and from there they soon found a trail in the grass that led to a nearby grassy knoll. Following the trail, they made their way across to the hill top, and were greatly surprised at what they found upon it. Maybe they were expecting to come across a ruffian sitting up there; at any rate it's probably fair to say they weren't expecting to find a very large serpent coiled up - seemingly asleep - in the warm summer sun.

While it may have appeared to be asleep, the snake - in fact - was far from it, and it soon rose upon being disturbed so rudely. It raised its head high in the air, hissing loudly, and lunging about in a threatening way; not that its aggressive and menacing behaviour (or its bulk) were to be of any use. The searchers just shot it dead. Once they were sure it was dead, they measured the snake and sliced open its enormously distended stomach, which was found to contain several birds including twites, buntings, pipits, larks and thrushes, and a vast amount of milk. It seems they had got their milk thief after all.

The Mull Dragon

If Mull wasn't troubled enough with faery hounds foretelling impending death and doom, (and who knows what mystery felids lurking in the hills, popping out every now and again to confound those watching), its waters might even contain the odd wandering mermaid. As well as these cryptids, there is also a tale of a dragon, and for the sake of completeness of mystery animal tales that abound in these isles, it has been included here. And when one has heard this story, it just might start to ring a couple of bells.

Long ago, back in the distant past, there resided a dragon on the island of Mull. Its lair could be found to the south of Loach Sguabain at *Beinn Fhada* (the long hill). Even today, the hill sports a hollow that was created by the beast as it crouched there on the lookout for dinner, which would mean it was looking for both the lonely traveller and any livestock that happened to be wandering past. It didn't take long for the ever-hungry dragon to clear the glen of all its livestock; and the numbers of lonely travellers became drastically reduced, as even the most unwary of them realised that a detour was preferable to becoming part of the dragon's lunch.

Eventually, it came to pass that the local king had had enough, and decided it was time to appeal for help. In time-honoured tradition, he offered the hand of his daughter, (and no doubt the rest of her as well, even if the tale doesn't go into too much detail on that subject), to the man who could rid his land of the dragon. The princess must have been a tempting lass, because there was no shortage of volunteers to go and face the beast at its lair at *Beinn Fhada*. Perhaps it was because their heads were full of lustful thoughts, or maybe it was just because the dragon was good at being a man-eating beast, that none of the would-be dragon slayers managed to cause it any more trouble than becoming stuck between its teeth.

No doubt by the process of natural selection, the quality of dragon slayers started to improve greatly by the time the last fellow came to give it a go. Perhaps it was because he was well aware of the previous unsuccessful slayers, and how their plans had ultimately failed. Or maybe he had been keeping a keen eye on how others had overcome similar challenges.

Sailing his ship up Loch Scridian, he anchored close to the shore, and rolled out a floating bridge of barrels that stretched all the way to the land. Once the barrels were in place he began setting sharp iron spikes into each one, ensuring that the wicked points faced upwards. It would be safe to say that health and safety officials would have thrown a fit if they had found out. After leaving the dangerous causeway, our young hero headed off in search of some of the remaining cattle, and soon enough he had managed to collect a small herd together. What their owners would have thought of this behaviour is only guesswork. Regardless of whether he got any permission to acquire the cattle, or had just stolen them he drove the beasts up towards the dragon's lair.

The dragon must have thought that it was its birthday when it spied all those potential meals walking up the glen towards it. Without giving it another moment's thought, it leapt from its lair, and raced down the glen towards the herd. Even with the dragon bounding down towards him, the young hero wasn't fazed. He was, after all, expecting this reaction. What the cattle made of it we don't know, but after the hero cut the throat of the animal nearest to the dragon, they probably had more pressing concerns on their minds. With the blood still dripping from his sword, the hero ushered the remaining animals back down the glen towards his ship where it lay at anchor, while behind them, the dragon started to tuck into the still-warm body of the slaughtered animal. After wolfing down the remains, the dragon set off once more down the glen in pursuit of the rest of the cattle. But before it could catch up with the main body of the herd, it came across yet another animal lying in a pool of its own blood; another sacrifice that had been recently slaughtered by the nameless hero (I wonder if he wore a poncho). Again, the dragon tucked into the free lunch before setting off once more in pursuit. This game of pursuit and free lunch would continue all the way down the glen towards the waiting ship. Maybe it was brilliant strategic planning, or maybe it was just pure jammy luck, but the last of the cattle met its grisly fate at the end of the hero's sword just before the start of the causeway. Having run out of cattle, there was nothing else for our hero to do but run for the safety of his ship (ensuring, of course, that he didn't come a cropper on his own careless metalwork that was sticking up from the floating barrels). It didn't take long for the dragon to finish off its last meal, and ever hungry, it would seem it bounded off towards the ship, eager to finish off the hero as dessert. So eager was the beast, that it didn't realise what peril the spiky barrels offered, and it didn't take long for it to come undone, skewered, kebab-style, on one of the wicked iron spikes that stuck proudly up from the barrels.

Once he was sure that the dragon was dead, the hero arranged for the corpse to be tied up, and proceeded to tow it along behind the ship all the way to the king. After all, if you are going to claim the king's daughter's hand you need some proof (the small print in these contracts can be devilish).

Now, doesn't that seem very similar to the tale of the dragon that was found on Islay, and how it met its fate at the hands, or rather at the barrels, of the local hero? Perhaps at one time the Inner Hebrides were plagued with a plethora of dragons whose presence attracted a number of dragon-slaying heroes who had barrels to spare. Or maybe it just points towards a shared Norse heritage of dragon-slaying tales.

APPENDIX I

Glossary of terms

Archelon ischyros: a turtle dating from the late Cretaceous period.

Aurora Borealis: the northern lights, streamers of coloured lights occasionally seen in the northern sky.

Black house: a traditional single story house with walls up to 6 feet thick and a low thatched roof. The type did not possess a chimney so smoke from the open fire would drift through the house. In earlier times the family would live in one end and the families' cattle at the other.

Bogha mem Crann: Stinky Bay, a rocky inlet on Benbecula so called because of fermenting seaweed that gathers there.

Bothy: a basic hut in a remote location.

Cait sith: faery cat, the size of large dog, black in colour with the exception of white markings on its chest. It may refer to early sightings of the Kellas cat.

Crò sith: faery cattle, said to be slightly smaller than highland cattle, also noted for the lack of any horns. Believed to live in the sea.

Cu sith: faery dog, a large mystery dog said to be the size of a two year old heifer and green in colour.

Dobhar-chu: Irish water hound. A very large mystery otter that has occasionally been known to kill people.

Each-uisge: water horse, a mystical animal that was said to haunt lonely stretches of water and lochs where it would waylay passers-by in the guise of a horse, it would entice people to mount it before dragging them into the loch to eat. It could also shape change into a little old lady.

Feolagan: an animal similar to a mouse that possessed the ability to paralyse sheep just by walking across the sheep's back.

Fiollan worm: a parasitic worm that lives between the flesh and the skin.

Gigelorum: a very small and almost certainly made up mystery creature that was said to make its nest in the ears of mites.

Globster: a virtually unidentifiable lump of rotting flesh washed up on beaches around the world, can measure up to 30 feet in length. While it could be the remains of an unknown sea creature it could also just as easily be the last dregs of a long dead whale that has washed ashore.

Guga: a young gannet hunted for food and reputed to taste like duck stewed in cod liver oil.

Kellas Cat: a hybrid of a Scottish wild cat and a domestic cat named after the village of Kellas. In appearance it is a large black cat and could be the source of the *Cait sith* tradition.

Kirk: the Church of Scotland or just a church.

Lochan: a small loch or tarn.

The Long Island: the name for the island that plays host to both Harris and Lewis.

Maighdean nan tonn: maiden of the waves, another name for a mermaid.

Manse: a house provided by the church for the minister.

Melonistic leopard: genetic melanism, a leopard having black fur instead of the normal colour.

Minch: the body of water that separates the Long Island from Skye and the mainland of Scotland.

Norwegian sea serpent: a snake-like sea serpent so named as for a long time the type was only spotted around the Norwegian coast.

Pinniped: from the Latin for 'fin footed' or 'wing footed', a term that encompasses true seal, fur seals and sea lion and not forgetting walrus.

Ph'nglui mglw'nafh Cthulhu R'lyeh wgah'nagl fhtagn : At his house in R'lyeh, dead Cthulhu waits dreaming. A rhyming couplet from the books of H.P. Lovecraft concerning an octopoid alien god who lives sleeping under the sea in some lost city. In some of Lovecraft's stories it is suggested that some of his undersea followers have connections with costal towns around the world.

Sea pork: a local seventeenth century term for whale meat.

Seileach uisge: water brute noted for both its repulsiveness and ferocity, possibly a giant eel that could once be found in the lonely lochs of Lewis. However the name translates literally as water snail, repulsive maybe, ferocious doubtful.

Shieling: the shelter or hut in which drovers, shepherds and others dwell when the cows are herded to the hills for summer grazing.

Sluagh: a faery hunting host that fly through the night sky towards the west following in the wild hunt tradition.

Sœneyti: in Icelandic folklore the sœneyti are a type of cow that lived under the sea and occasionally came on land, caught by cunning herdsmen. In many ways similar to the *crò sith*.

Taghairm: a dark ritual involving the torture of cats done to gain an audience with a demon cat that would grant the torturer wishes.

Tarbh-uisge: water bull, generally believed to live in lonely lochs and pools, the black bull-like animal occasionally comes on land to mate with nearby cows. Said to possess the horns of a true bull but lacks any trace of ears.

Tir-nan-Og: the land of the ever young, a mystical land to the west over the Atlantic Ocean, said to be the final destination of the *Sluagh*.

Zooform: a term used to describe things that appear to be real flesh and blood animals but are not. Sightings of ghostly dogs would fit into this category.

APPENDIX II

Spotters guide

I have long thought that books should not be just a static display to be read just the once, and left to pass the rest of their lives sad on a book case gathering dust to the end of their days. To me a book is a living depository of knowledge that is there to be used and abused, and lives a short happy life out in the countryside. I remember as a little lad taking my father's old aircraft recognition book on trips out to the local air shows in the 1970s and 80s, and boy does that copy show it now - spine shattered and pages falling out*.

You might wonder the point of that, well it is simply this, I had great fun looking up into the skies watching those old aircraft fly by (and occasionally crashing it has to be added), all the time I would be eagerly flicking through that tattered old book looking for the last plane that had flown past or seeing what plane I would like to see go by. It brought the world of vintage aircraft to life and with that in mind I would like to present you with this, the spotters guide to the Mystery Animals of the Western Isles. After all if you get out to the Western Isles why not take this book with you, you never know what you might stumble across.

* You will be glad to know while the original book died happy another copy was bought some years later to replace it.

Contents of Spotters Guide

Big Cat
Black Dog
Cu sith
Dragon
Each-uisge as Little Old Lady
Each-uisge as Water horse
Faery Cow
Feolagan
Fiollan worm
Giant Turtle
Globster
Great Auk
King Otter
Long-Necked Sea Serpent
Many-Humped Sea Serpent
Merhorse
Mermaid
Milk Stealing Snake
Seal Folk
Sluagh Hunting Dog
Water Bull
Water Horse
Werewolf

Big Cat

What is it?
A large mystery feline, one of many sightings reported in the United Kingdom. At least one of the sightings from Mull certainly suggests that the animal in question may be a puma, while other reports from Mull describe a large black cat perhaps a melanistic leopard or possibly some as yet unknown native cat perhaps the very animal the *Cait sith* is based upon.

Where has it been seen?
Reports of big cat sights are so far restricted to three locations. In July 1999 the island of Colonsay provided a single sighting of a large cat, in 2007 the isle of Skye provided a sighting. But the isle of Mull is the place to go if you want to see a big cats, with a tradition of sightings going back to the late 1970s big cats have been reported in both the Loch na Keal and Craignure areas of the island.

What to look for
Try a big cat far in excess of the average domestic cat, for example if the cat in question was a melanistic leopard you could be looking at one measuring up to 6½ feet in length and weighing in at up to 200lbs. You are more likely to come across paw marks or scratch marks on trees than the actual cat, while not as impressive as a sighting of the animal they are still important evidence in the quest for identify this unknown cat.

What to do if you see one
If it is safe try and take a picture. It is advisable not to approach the animal but rather just to observe from where you are, still it might be worth keeping your fingers crossed it heads away from you, most reports suggest that they will leave with no interaction. Once the animal has gone it might be worthwhile to take a few photographs of any prints left.

Worth considering
It is possible to confuse a large domestic cat in the quest for this mystery cat especially if the sighting is at a distance it can become hard to gauge the scale easily.

Had a sighting?
If so fill your notes in here.

Black Dog

What is it?
The phantom black dog appears to be a spectral omen of doom; it may be a zooform creature or could be based on early misidentified black cats.

Where has it been seen?
The Black Dog of Ardura was said to haunt the area around Lochbuie House on Mull. It was often seen by the good Dr. Reginald MacDonald which certainly seemed to finish off a number of his patients.

What to look for
It appears that no matter how hard you look the phantom black dog will only put in an appearance when someone is at death's door and even then it only seems to appear to those gifted with second sight.

What to do if you see one
Keep your fingers crossed that it isn't looking for you.

Worth considering
If you happen to be in Mull and catch a glimpse of a large black animal in the distance or hiding in a bush it might be worth considering that the animal is actually the famed big cat of Mull.

Had a sighting?
If so fill your notes in here.

Cu sith

<u>What is it?</u>
A very good question, most likely some kind of zooform creature, but the possibility that it could be based on mystery cat sightings or a folk memory of wolves should not be discounted.

<u>Where has it been seen?</u>
These canine critters have been seen all over the isles from leaving teeth in spuds on Lewis, invisibly walking along Harris beaches, terrorizing Tiree and not forgetting startling people after midnight.

<u>What to look for</u>
If you are on Harris look for big paw prints in the sand (remember stepping in them could lead to madness). If elsewhere look for either a great hound the size of a large heifer or a collie sized white dog

<u>What to do if you see one</u>
First of all get those pictures taken and if you are walking on Luskentyre beach when you see it give yourself a pat on the back, it's usually invisible. Evidence from South Uist suggests that you won't have to get out of its path as it will walk right through you. But one thing that all sources agree on is that if it starts barking you don't want to hang around for the third bark.

<u>Worth considering</u>
It is worth considering that the *cu sith* in front of you might just be a dog.

<u>Had a sighting?</u>
If so fill your notes in here.

Dragon

What is it?
A great flying monster, possibly a flying reptile.

Where has it been seen?
Back in the darkest days of the Middle Ages the Inner Hebrides seemed to be the place to find them, in Mull the haunt was south of Loach Sguabain at *Beinn Fhada*, it also seems to have had a twin on Islay.

What to look for
Terrorized peasants pleading for help, smoking ruins and devoured livestock.

What to do if you see one
Get those photographs taken before tricking it into running over spiked barrels that you have left cunningly in place, before claiming your handsome reward.

Worth considering
Look to the skies for something unexpected flying by.

Had a sighting?
If so fill your notes in here.

Each-uisge as Little Old Lady

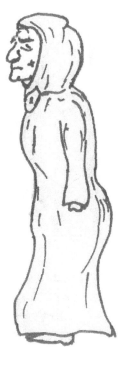

<u>What is it?</u>
One of the many guises that the shape-shifting *each-uisge* used to trick
its way into gaining entry to your home before feasting on members of
your family. Some people may say that it is just a device used to ex
plain the danger of strangers.

<u>Where has it been seen?</u>
On the isle of Lewis on the outskirts of the village of Shawbost.

<u>What to look for</u>
A crinkled old crone suddenly appearing, possibly with a piece of pond
weed sticking out from her hair.

<u>What to do if you see one</u>
Keep your eye on her and don't let her in whatever you do.

<u>Worth considering</u>
Easily mistaken for a genuine little old lady.

<u>Had a sighting?</u>
If so fill your notes in here.

Each-uisge as Water horse

What is it?
A mysterious carnivorous aquatic animal that appears to haunt lonely lochs and lochans. Traditional stories suggest that it would appear on the shore in the guise of a friendly pony or well dressed horse, it would use this look to entice people to mount it, once on board they would be unable to climb off and be dragged into the water to be drowned and then eaten by the *each-uisge*. It is possible that the stories of the *each-uisge* started as a way to warn youngsters of the dangers of drowning in still waters.

Where has it been seen?
It has been recorded in a number of places on the isle of Skye, one sighting in the region of Uig.

What to look for
A very innocent looking pony standing by the shore of a lonely loch, possibly there might be a piece of liver washed up nearby.

What to do if you see one
By all means take photographs; even feed it a sugar lump or two. Just don't mount it.

Worth considering
It could easily be mistaken for a normal pony.

Had a sighting?
If so fill your notes in here.

Faery Cow

What is it?
A small cow that spends most of its time living beneath the sea occasionally coming ashore. It resembles the usual highland cattle but lacks any trace of horns.

Where has it been seen?
Reports have been made in the region of Luskentyre in Harris as well as on Skye.

What to look for
A herd of cows coming out of the sea and wandering ashore to go grazing.

What to do if you see one
Get those pictures taken as it emerges out of the surf they might make a few quid. If you fancy keeping it for your own herd try blocking its route back into the sea, it might work.

Worth considering
The cow in the surf could easily be a normal cow that is fond of eating seaweed.

Had a sighting?
If so fill your notes in here.

Feolagan

What is it?
A mystery mouse-like animal.

Where has it been seen?
On the hills around Kebock Head on the isle of Lewis, failing that try any Hebridean moor.

What to look for
A good clue is to start looking for a paralyzed sheep standing still in the middle of a field.

What to do if you see one
If you happen to own a sheep that has recently and mysteriously become paralyzed catch hold of the feolagan and get it to walk across the back of your sheep, it should free the animal up. Even if you don't have any sheep at risk try and get a photograph of it, I for one am very curious to know what one looks like.

Worth considering
A mystery mouse-like animal acting suspiciously around a field of sheep.

Had a sighting?
If so fill your notes in here.

Fiollan worm

What is it?
A horrible little parasitic worm.

Where has it been seen?
In the Middle Ages it was famed
for its presence on Skye, just look
between the skin and the flesh.

What to look for
Random bruising and the suspicion
that there is something crawling
under your skin.

What to do if you see one
If it's on you try and find a doctor and keep your fingers crossed it hasn't start to lay those eggs.

Worth considering
Look out for people with grubby nails trying to force it out of the skin.

Had a sighting?
If so fill your notes in here.

Giant Turtle

What is it?
A mystery giant sea turtle with an estimated length stretching from 15 feet up to 40 feet. A possible descendant of the prehistoric turtle the *Archelon ischyros* a turtle dating from the late Cretaceous period that measured 12 feet long with a circumference of 25 feet.

Where has it been seen?
In 1959 the shark fisherman Tex Geddes and his companion spotted just such a large turtle swimming in the waters off the isle of Soay in the Inner Hebrides.

What to look for
A very large turtle slowly swimming by.

What to do if you see one
Take a few photos if possible trying to get some item of known length in the picture for size comparison.

Worth considering
The type could be confused with sightings of the leatherback turtle which has not only been recorded as growing up to 9 feet in length but can also be found in the waters around the Hebrides.

Had a sighting?
If so fill your notes in here.

Globster

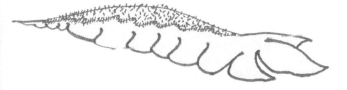

What is it?
A large lump of putrescent flesh that at first glance offers no clue as to what it had been in life.

Where has it been seen?
A well reported example was washed ashore on the island of Benbecula in 1990.

What to look for
You will probably smell it long before you see it. You are looking for a large lump of rotting tissue.

What to do if you see one
Hold your nose and take a picture or two. Probably best not to touch it nor would it seem a good idea to have a picnic lunch down wind of it.

Worth considering
While a globster is a large lump of unidentified flesh, there are of course plenty of large identifiable lumps of dead animal that wash ashore on a regular basis and they all smell equally as bad.

Had a sighting?
If so fill your notes in here.

Great Auk

What is it?
A large flightless bird which resembled the southern hemisphere's penguin in its behaviour. Almost certainly extinct since the last two died on the Icelandic island of Eldey in 1844. Also known by the name Garefowl.

Where has it been seen?
One definite sighting was on the rocky outcrop of Stac-an-Armin one of the St Kilda group of islands. It is possible that two further birds were observed and later shot on the Skye in the 1850s.

What to look for
A flightless sea bird with striking black and white plumage and a large beak.

What to do if you see one
Don't beat it to death thinking it is a storm witch, and come to think of it don't go shooting it either. Take a few pictures and stand back amazed at your sighting.

Worth considering
It is vaguely similar in shape, size and colouration to the great northern diver, this similarity could give a false sighting.

Had a sighting?
If so fill your notes in here.

King Otter

What is it?
The king otter is a larger than average otter, that according to some would be found at the head of a procession of seven others of its kind. Its skin was once favoured as a means of protecting the owner from bullets, luckily there is now a wide range of body armour.

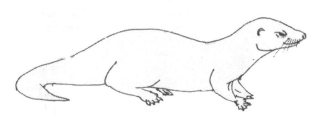

Where has it been seen?
A true mystery that question. It was stated to be rare in the sixteenth century but could still be lurking somewhere in the Western Isles. I realize that is vague but so are the reports of the animal.

What to look for
A large otter that has a single white spot about the size of a five pence piece upon its breast. With the exception of that white spot it is rumoured to be bullet proof, but kindly note that shooting otters to find a king otter is not to be attempted.

What to do if you see one
Get those photographs taken.

Worth considering
Understandably it is easy to confuse sights of normal otters for this extraordinary animal.

Had a sighting?
If so fill your notes in here

Long-necked sea serpent

What is it?
One of the all time sea serpent greats with sightings recorded from all across the world's oceans. The origin of this mystery beast has been suggested as an unknown type of pinniped. Reported to measure from 15 to 60 feet in length, its most famous feature of course is its long neck, this along with the lack of a mane separates the type from the merhorse.

Where has it been seen?
Some time around the start of the twentieth century sightings of the type occurred off the coast of Skye, possibly attracted to the area following a seasonal bounty of fish.

What to look for
A long neck possibly in the region of twenty feet long appearing out of the sea.

What to do if you see one
It depends on where you are, if on shore try and take a photograph, if you are at sea the traditional response is to head for shore at high speed.

Worth considering
Could be mistaken at a distance for a merhorse and equally it would also seem easy to confuse it with a submarine.

Had a sighting?
If so fill your notes in here.

Many-humped sea serpent

What is it?
A large mystery animal measuring between 60 and 100 feet long, features a medium length neck. Both recognized and named after its many humps that often show above the water's surface. The type seems to occupy a range that stretches across the North Atlantic.

Where has it been seen?
One cruised up and down the Sound of Sleat in 1872 seemingly trying its hardest to attract the attention of Messrs Macrea and Twopeny on their sailing holiday.

What to look for
A row of humps stretching across the water as the animal gently cruises by.

What to do if you see one
As with all larger mystery sea serpents there seems to be two schools of thought, one is to sit back and watch it go by whereas the second approach is to head for the hills.

Worth considering
Daft as is it might sound the sighting of many humps in the sea does not necessarily equate to the sighting of a many-humped sea serpent, it could just as easily be a line of dolphins or even seals swimming along in formation.

Had a sighting?
If so fill your notes in here.

Merhorse

What is it?
One of the all time sea serpent greats with sightings recorded from all the world's oceans. The origin of this mystery beast has been suggested as an unknown type of pinniped. With a body length measuring between 15 to 100 feet long and with a camel-like head, a flowing mane and not forgetting a pair of very large eyes.

Where has it been seen?
The best recorded sighting in the area took place in June 1808 off the coast of Coll.

What to look for
While looking out to sea the sudden arrival of a small island from the depths that in turn suddenly produces a neck should be a good clue.

What to do if you see one
The standard response on encountering such a creature was to head for shore at all speed, there is a strong suspicion that the type may not be averse to munching on people. Of course if you feel safe to do so get some photographs taken you never know it could make you famous.

Worth considering
It could in theory be mistaken for a long-necked sea serpent but hey if you spot one of those instead don't worry it's still a good result.

Had a sighting?
If so fill your notes in here.

Mermaid

What is it?
Traditional stories tell of a creature that possesses the upper body of a woman with the lower half being that of a fish. There are several theories as to what the mermaid could be ranging from an as yet unidentified seal which could pass for human at a distance to an unknown aquatic ape.

Where has it been seen?
Over the years there have been a number of sightings in the Western Isles from Benbecula, South Uist, Barra right up to the last reported sighting from Muck in 1947.

What to look for
If you have a keen eye why not scan the shoreline for any sign of a topless woman sat on the rock with her lower body dangling into the sea while she combs her hair. If staring at the sea doesn't take your fancy why not head to Benbecula and try your luck at trying to find the mermaid's grave in Nunton graveyard, until the 1960s it was supposedly easy to find.

What to do if you see one
Get the camera out and take a few photos, don't throw stones at her.

Worth considering
Don't be tempted by the mermaid's charms, tradition is that she will attempt to drag you into the sea for who knows what.

Had a sighting?
If so fill your notes in here.

Milk stealing snake

What is it?
A large snake measuring around 9 feet in length with a fondness for milk.

Where has it been seen?
In the nineteenth century a snake fitting this description was killed at Bailemonaidh on Islay.

What to look for
If you notice that something has been at your milk store look for the give away trail of milk that will lead all the way to the snake.

What to do if you see one
Take a few pictures and consider not leaving your milk outdoors in future.

Worth considering
Your missing milk could be as a result of a human milk thief.

Had a sighting?
If so fill your notes in here.

Seal Folk

What is it?
A seal that rather bizarrely seems to contain
a person within it skin, a person that occasionally pops out for a bit of fresh air usually leaving the seal skin carelessly lying
about nearby.

Where has it been seen?
Ancient reports from both North Uist and
Colonsay.

What to look for
Seal skins piled up on a beach where a
group of naked people are to be seen dancing in the moonlight.

What to do if you see one
If you're lonely and can't afford a mail order bride steal a skin and wait at home for a
naked seal woman to turn up wanting to be
your wife. It's worth considering that she
will of course eventually find her missing seal skin and once found she will head back to sea taking any
children with her.

Worth considering
Naked people dancing could just be naturists.

Had a sighting?
If so fill your notes in here.

Sluagh Hunting Dog

What is it?
The spectral hunting hound of that spirit host of the northern skies the *Sluagh*. What these hounds are hunting for is a mystery but with their faery masters directing them would it be too hard to imagine that it's humans.

Where has it been seen?
Usually racing across the northern skies heading towards Tir-nan-Og in the far west. Occasionally they make a touch down and such a sighting was made in Benbecula when a couple of hounds popped into a hovel.

What to look for
An unusual looking hound that has a bejeweled collar and leash.

What to do if you see one
If you want a quiet life hide in a corner and whimper, if you fancy a short but wonderful life of constant travelling across the heavens follow the dog out to its masters and see if there is a vacancy in the *Sluagh*.

Worth considering
The *Sluagh* were renowned for their cruelty so it possibly isn't such a good idea to go and ask for that lift after all.

Had a sighting?
If so fill your notes in here.

Water Bull

What is it?
A mystery bull-like animal occasionally going by the name *tarbh uisge*
that makes its home near lonely lochs
and lochans.

Where has it been seen?
A number of reports have been made
on the isle of St Kilda.

What to look for
A bull small in size with a nice set of
horns but rather tellingly it has no ears.

What to do if you see one
Take a few pictures and it you own
any cows try and keep them away
from it as it will try its luck with the
ladies.

Worth considering
Not to mistake this benign happy little fellow for the altogether much nastier *each-uisge*.

Had a sighting?
If so fill your notes in here.

Water horse

What is it?
The real deal, none of this shape-changing malarkey for this animal, it is real flesh and blood. It is possible that the sightings are based on out of place seals or walrus but then again who really knows what really lurks in those lonely lochs.

Where has it been seen?
A good sighting occurred on the shores of Loch Duvat on the isle of Eriskay in 1893.

What to look for
A strange looking animal with a passing resemblance to a dead cow. Likely to be spotted either swimming in a loch or at the side of the loch minding its own business.

What to do if you see one
Get you camera out and get those photographs taken, it might be worthwhile keeping your distance mind you, it might be as hungry as the dreaded *each-uisge*.

Worth considering
If your mystery animal on the loch shore looks like a dead cow and if as you get closer to it you notice that you disturb a large number of flies and there is a nasty smell in the air the chances are you have found a dead cow.

Had a sighting?
If so fill your notes in here.

Werewolf

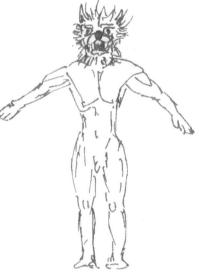

What is it?
A legendary dog-headed human, to some it is a shape shifter to others it is nothing more than a folk memory of a time when wolves roamed around the countryside.

Where has it been seen?
Somewhere in the Hebrides around the reign of Queen Victoria. A possible location has been given as Loch Langavat but which one of them is hard to say. Following the tradition of the British werewolf it will make an appearance at any kitchen window where its last mortal remains are laid out on the kitchen table.

What to look for
In general a wolf-headed human. In terms of the Hebridean werewolf look for a shallow grave containing the skull of a wolf upon the skeleton of a human. Once found just take it home and leave the bones on the kitchen table, expect a visit that evening.

What to do if you see one
If you feel safe take a picture, if not try running in the opposite direction. If your sighting is a late night visit in response to you taking the bones home, just barricade the door, do something else in another room and ensure you rebury those bones the next morning.

Worth considering
Watch out for a human skeleton with a wolf's skull on top.

Had a sighting?
If so fill your notes in here.

BIBLIOGRAPHY

Arnold, Neil *Monster The A-Z of Zooform Phenomena* (CFZ Press, 2007)

BBC News Scotland website 12/12/08

Clutton-Brock, Juliet *Mammals* (Dorling Kindersley, London, 2002)

Coleman, Loren & Huyghe, Patrick *The field guide to Bigfoot & other mystery primates* (Anomalist Books, San Antonio, 2006)

Costello, Peter *In Search of Lake Monsters* (Garnstone Press, 1974)

Big Cats in Britain Yearbook 2007 (CFZ Press)

Big Cats in Britain Yearbook 2008 (CFZ Press)

Downes Jonathan (ed) *The Centre for Fortean Zoology Yearbook 2007* (CFZ Press, 2007)

Downes, Jonathan & Freeman, Richard (eds) *The Centre for Fortean Zoology Yearbook 2000/1* (CFZ Press, 2008)

Downes, Jonathan & Freeman, Richard (eds) *The Centre for Fortean Zoology Yearbook 2002* (CFZ Press, 2007)

Downes, Jonathan & Freeman, Richard (eds) *The Centre for Fortean Zoology Yearbook 2003* (CFZ Press, 2008)

Downes, Jonathan & Inglis, Graham (eds) *The Centre for Fortean Zoology Yearbook 1998* (CFZ Press, 2008)

Eberhart, George M. *Mysterious Creatures* (ABC-CLIO, Inc., 2002)
Freeman, Richard *Dragons: More than a Myth* (CFZ Press, 2005)

Fuller, Errol *The Great Auk* (Errol Fuller, 1999)

Gaskell, Jeremy *Who killed the Great Auk?* (Oxford University Press, 2000)

Hall, Jamie *Half Human Half Animal Tales of Werewolves and Related Creatures* (1st books, Bloomington IN, 2003)

Harpur, Merrily *Mystery big cats* (Heart of Albion, 2006, Loughborough)

Harte, Jeremy *Explore Fairy Traditions* (Explore Books an imprint of Albion Press, 2004)

Harvie-Brown, J.A. & Buckley, T.E. *A Vertebrate Fauna of the Outer Hebrides* (Edinburgh, 1888 (MDCCCLXXXVIII))

Heuvelmans, Bernard *In the wake of the sea serpents* (Hill & Wang, 1968)

Jones, David S.D. *Game on Lewis and Harris – past and present* (Islands Book Trust, 2007)

Lucas, Bill *Dateline Stornoway* (Hebridean Press Service, 2008)

MacGregor, Alasdair Alpin *The Ghost Book* (Robert Hale, 1955)

MacGregor, Alasdair Alpin *The Haunted Isles* (Alexander Maclehose & Co, 1933)

MacGregor, Alasdair Alpin *Peat Fire Flame* (The Ettrick Press, London, 1947)

MacGregor, Alasdair Alpin *Strange Tales of the Highlands & Islands* (Lang Syne)

Mackenzie, Donald Alexander *Wonder Tales from Scottish Myth and Legend* (1917)

Macnab, P.A. *The Isle of Mull* (David & Charles, 1970)

Matthews, Marcus *Big Cats loose in Britain* (CFZ Press, 2007)

Maxwell, Gavin *Harpoon at a venture* (Rupert Hart-Davies, London, 1955)

Morrison, Norman *Hebridean Lore & Romance* (Inverness, 1936)

Newton, Michael *Encyclopeadia of Cryptozoology a global guide* (Macfarland & Company Inc, Jefferson, 2005)

Maclellan Angus, translated by John Lorne Campbell *Stories from South Uist* (Routledge Kegan Paul, London, 1961)

Oudemans, A.C. *The great sea serpent* (Cosimo Classics, New York, 2007)

Penrith, James & Deborah *The Western Isles* (vacation work, 2002)

Reader's Digest *Folklore, Myths and Legends* (Reader's Digest, 1973)

Reeves, Randall R. Stewart, Brent S., Clapham, Philip J., Powell, James A. *Sea Mammals of the World* (A & C Black, London, 2002)

Shuker, Dr Karl P.N. *Dr Shuker's casebook in pursuit of marvels and mysteries* (CFZ Press, 2008)

Shuker, Dr Karl P.N. *The beasts that hide from man, seeking the world's last undiscovered animals*

The Mystery Animals of the Western Isles

(Paraview Press, New York, 2003)

Swire, Otta F.*The Outer Hebrides & their Legends* (Oliver & Boyd 1966)

Whitaker, Terence *Scotland's Ghosts and Apparitions* (Hale, 1991)

Woodley, Michael A. *In the Wake of Bernard Heuvelmans* (CFZ Press, 2008)

Zell-Ravenheart, Oberon & DeKirk, Ash 'LeopardDancer' *A wizards bestiary* (The Career Press inc, 2007)

Glen Vaudrey

The author was born into a dying farming community in Lancashire in 1972, the eldest son of farm labourers.

He spent a decade travelling the more remote parts of northern and Eastern Europe during which time he worked variously as a court usher, regularly cooked breakfast for 70, farmed snails, and at one low point was to be found cleaning public toilets (at least that job came with a pair of Marigold gloves), and despite this has become an authority on Iron Age coinage.

Having spent the last three years living in a stable in the Outer Hebrides he has finally settled down on the border of Cheshire where he revels in the title of a natural mystic.

INDEX

THE CENTRE FOR FORTEAN ZOOLOGY

So, what is the Centre for Fortean Zoology?

We are a non profit-making organisation founded in 1992 with the aim of being a clearing house for information, and coordinating research into mystery animals around the world. We also study out of place animals, rare and aberrant animal behaviour, and Zooform Phenomena; little-understood "things" that appear to be animals, but which are in fact nothing of the sort, and not even alive (at least in the way we understand the term).

Why should I join the Centre for Fortean Zoology?

Not only are we the biggest organisation of our type in the world, but - or so we like to think - we are the best. We are certainly the only truly global Cryptozoological research organisation, and we carry out our investigations using a strictly scientific set of guidelines. We are expanding all the time and looking to recruit new members to help us in our research into mysterious animals and strange creatures across the globe. Why should you join us? Because, if you are genuinely interested in trying to solve the last great mysteries of Mother Nature, there is nobody better than us with whom to do it.

What do I get if I join the Centre for Fortean Zoology?

For £12 a year, you get a four-issue subscription to our journal *Animals & Men*. Each issue contains 60 pages packed with news, articles, letters, research papers, field reports, and even a gossip column! The magazine is A5 in format with a full colour cover. You also have access to one of the world's largest collections of resource material dealing with cryptozoology and allied disciplines, and people from the CFZ membership regularly take part in fieldwork and expeditions around the world.

How is the Centre for Fortean Zoology organized?

The CFZ is managed by a three-man board of trustees, with a non-profit making trust registered with HM Government Stamp Office. The board of trustees is supported by a Permanent Directorate of full and part-time staff, and advised by a Consultancy Board of specialists - many of whom who are world-renowned experts in their particular field. We have regional representatives across the UK, the USA, and many other parts of the world, and are affiliated with other organisations whose aims and protocols mirror our own.

I am new to the subject, and although I am interested I have little practical knowledge. I don't want to feel out of my depth. What should I do?

Don't worry. We were *all* beginners once. You'll find that the people at the CFZ are friendly and approachable. We have a thriving forum on the website which is the hub of an ever-growing electronic community. You will soon find your feet. Many members of the CFZ Permanent Directorate started off as ordinary members, and now work full-time chasing monsters around the world.

I have an idea for a project which isn't on your website. What do I do?

Write to us, e-mail us, or telephone us. The list of future projects on the website is not exhaustive. If you have a good idea for an investigation, please tell us. We may well be able to help.

How do I go on an expedition?

We are always looking for volunteers to join us. If you see a project that interests you, do not hesitate to get in touch with us. Under certain circumstances we can help provide funding for your trip. If you look on the future projects section of the website, you can see some of the projects that we have pencilled in for the next few years.

In 2003 and 2004 we sent three-man expeditions to Sumatra looking for Orang-Pendek - a semi legendary bipedal ape. The same three went to Mongolia in 2005. All three members started off merely subscribers to the CFZ magazine.

Next time it could be you!

Project Kerinci, Sumatra - 2003
In search of the bipedal ape Orang Pendek

How is the Centre for Fortean Zoology funded?

We have no magic sources of income. All our funds come from donations, membership fees, works that we do for TV, radio or magazines, and sales of our publications and merchandise. We are always looking for corporate sponsorship, and other sources of revenue. If you have any ideas for fund-raising please let us know. However, unlike other cryptozoological organisations in the past, we do not live in an intellectual ivory tower. We are not afraid to get our hands dirty, and furthermore we are not one of those organisations where the membership have to raise money so that a privileged few can go on expensive foreign trips. Our research teams both in the UK and abroad, consist of a mixture of experienced and inexperienced personnel. We are truly a community, and work on the premise that the benefits of CFZ membership are open to all.

What do you do with the data you gather from your investigations and expeditions?

Reports of our investigations are published on our website as soon as they are available. Preliminary reports are posted within days of the project finishing.

Each year we publish a 200 page yearbook containing research papers and expedition report too long to be printed in the journal. We freely circulate our information to anybody who asks for it.

Is the CFZ community purely an electronic one?

No. Each year since 2000 we have held our annual convention - the *Weird Weekend* - in Exeter. It is three days of lectures, workshops, and excursions. But most importantly it is a chance for members of the CFZ to meet each other, and to talk with the members of the permanent directorate in a relaxed and informal setting and preferably with a pint of beer in one hand. Since 2006 - the *Weird Weekend* has been bigger and better and held in the idyllic rural location of Woolsery in North Devon. The 2008 event will be held over the weekend 15-17 August.

Since relocating to North Devon in 2005 we have become ever more closely involved with other community organisations, and we hope that this trend will continue. We also work closely with Police Forces across the UK as consultants for animal mutilation cases, and we intend to forge closer links with the coastguard and other community services. We want to work closely with those who regularly travel into the Bristol Channel, so that if the recent trend of exotic animal visitors to our coastal waters continues, we can be out there as soon as possible.

We are building a Visitor's Centre in rural North Devon. This will not be open to the general public, but will provide a museum, a library and an educational resource for our members (currently over 400) across the globe. We are also planning a youth organisation which will involve children and young people in our activities. We work closely with *Tropiquaria* - a small zoo in north Somerset, and have several exciting conservation projects planned.

Apart from having been the only Fortean Zoological organisation in the world to have consistently published material on all aspects of the subject for over a decade, we have achieved the following concrete results:

Disproved the myth relating to the headless so-called sea-serpent carcass of Durgan beach in Cornwall 1975
Disproved the story of the 1988 puma skull of Lustleigh Cleave
Carried out the only in-depth research ever into the mythos of the Cornish Owlman
Made the first records of a tropical species of lamprey
Made the first records of a luminous cave gnat larva in Thailand.
Discovered a possible new species of British mammal - the beech marten.
In 1994-6 carried out the first archival fortean zoological survey of Hong Kong.
In the year 2000, CFZ theories where confirmed when an entirely new species of lizard was found resident in Britain.
Identified the monster of Martin Mere in Lancashire as a giant wels catfish
Expanded the known range of Armitage's skink in the Gambia by 80%
Obtained photographic evidence of the remains of Europe's largest known pike
Carried out the first ever in-depth study of the *ninki-nanka*
Carried out the first attempt to breed Puerto Rican cave snails in captivity
Were the first European explorers to visit the `lost valley` in Sumatra
Published the first ever evidence for a new tribe of pygmies in Guyana
Published the first evidence for a new species of caiman in Guyana

EXPEDITIONS & INVESTIGATIONS TO DATE INCLUDE:

- 1998 Puerto Rico, Florida, Mexico *(Chupacabras)*
- 1999 Nevada *(Bigfoot)*
- 2000 Thailand *(The naga)*
- 2002 Martin Mere *(Giant catfish)*
- 2002 Cleveland *(Wallaby mutilation)*
- 2003 Bolam Lake *(BHM Reports)*
- 2003 Sumatra *(Orang Pendek)*
- 2003 Texas *(Bigfoot; giant snapping turtles)*
- 2004 Sumatra *(Orang Pendek; cigau, a sabre-toothed cat)*
- 2004 Illinois *(Black panthers; cicada swarm)*
- 2004 Texas *(Mystery blue dog)*
- 2004 Puerto Rico *(Chupacabras; carnivorous cave snails)*
- 2005 Belize *(Affiliate expedition for hairy dwarfs)*
- 2005 Mongolia *(Allghoi Khorkhoi aka Mongolian death worm)*
- 2006 Gambia *(Gambo - Gambian sea monster , Ninki Nanka and Armitage s skink*
- 2006 Llangorse Lake *(Giant pike, giant eels)*
- 2006 Windermere *(Giant eels)*
- 2007 Coniston Water *(Giant eels)*
- 2007 Guyana *(Giant anaconda, didi, water tiger)*
- 2008 Russia *(Almasty, giant snakes)*

To apply for a **FREE** information pack about th organisation and details of how to join, plus in formation on current and future projects, exped tions and events.

Send a stamped and addressed envelope to:

THE CENTRE FOR FORTEAN ZOOLOG MYRTLE COTTAGE, WOOLSERY, BIDEFORD, NORTH DEVON EX39 5QR.

or alternatively visit our website at:
w w w . c f z . o r g . u k

THE CENTRE FOR FORTEAN ZOOLOGY
www.cfz.org.uk

MYSTERY ANIMALS OF THE BRITISH ISLES

This is a major new series from CFZ Press. It will cover Great Britain and the Republic of Ireland, on a county by county basis, describing the mystery animals of the entire island group.

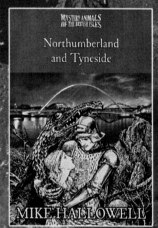

MYSTERY ANIMALS OF THE BRITISH ISLES

Northumberland and Tyneside

MIKE HALLOWELL

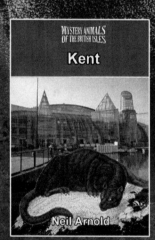

MYSTERY ANIMALS OF THE BRITISH ISLES

Kent

Neil Arnold

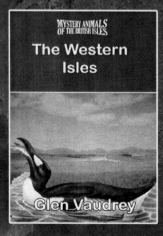

MYSTERY ANIMALS OF THE BRITISH ISLES

The Western Isles

Glen Vaudrey

Dr Karl Shuker is perhaps Britain's best loved, and most respected cryptozoological writer. CFZ Press are proud to be publishing a series of his books, mixing new titles with updated reissues of his classic works.....

Books available from
CFZ PRESS

CFZ PRESS

Other books available from
CFZ PRESS

CFZ PRESS

ONLY FOOLS AND GOATSUCKERS
Jonathan Downes - ISBN 0-9512872-3-0

£12.50

In January and February 1998 Jonathan Downes and Graham Inglis of the Centre for Fortean Zoology spent three and a half weeks in Puerto Rico, Mexico and Florida, accompanied by a film crew from UK Channel 4 TV. Their aim was to make a documentary about the terrifying chupacabra - a vampiric creature that exists somewhere in the grey area between folklore and reality. This remarkable book tells the gripping, sometimes scary, and often hilariously funny story of how the boys from the CFZ did their best to subvert the medium of contemporary TV documentary making and actually do their job.

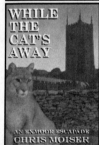

WHILE THE CAT'S AWAY
Chris Moiser - ISBN: 0-9512872-1-4

£7.99

Over the past thirty years or so there have been numerous sightings of large exotic cats, including black leopards, pumas and lynx, in the South West of England. Former Rhodesian soldier Sam McCall moved to North Devon and became a farmer and pub owner when Rhodesia became Zimbabwe in 1980. Over the years despite many of his pub regulars having seen the "Beast of Exmoor" Sam wasn't at all sure that it existed. Then a series of happenings made him change his mind. Chris Moiser—a zoologist—is well known for his research into the mystery cats of the westcountry. This is his first novel.

CFZ EXPEDITION REPORT 2006 - GAMBIA
ISBN 1905723032

£12.50

In July 2006, The J.T.Downes memorial Gambia Expedition - a six-person team - Chris Moiser, Richard Freeman, Chris Clarke, Oll Lewis, Lisa Dowley and Suzi Marsh went to the Gambia, West Africa. They went in search of a dragon-like creature, known to the natives as `Ninki Nanka`, which has terrorized the tiny African state for generations, and has reportedly killed people as recently as the 1990s. They also went to dig up part of a beach where an amateur naturalist claims to have buried the carcass of a mysterious fifteen foot sea monster named 'Gambo', and they sought to find the Armitage's Skink (*Chalcides armitagei*) - a tiny lizard first described in 1922 and only rediscovered in 1989. Here, for the first time, is their story.... With an forward by Dr. Karl Shuker and introduction by Jonathan Downes.

BIG CATS IN BRITAIN YEARBOOK 2006
Edited by Mark Fraser - ISBN 978-1905723-01-0

£10.00

Big cats are said to roam the British Isles and Ireland even now as you are sitting and reading this. People from all walks of life encounter these mysterious felines on a daily basis in every nook and cranny of these two countries. Most are jet-black, some white, some are brown, in fact big cats of every description and colour are seen by some unsuspecting person while on his or her daily business. 'Big Cats in Britain' are the largest and most active group in the British Isles and Ireland This is their first book. It contains a run-down of every known big cat sighting in the UK during 2005, together with essays by various luminaries of the British big cat research community which place the phenomenon into scientific, cultural, and historical perspective.

**CFZ PRESS, MYRTLE COTTAGE,
WOOLSERY, BIDEFORD,
NORTH DEVON, EX39 5QR
w w w . c f z . o r g . u k**

Other books available from
CFZ PRESS

CFZ PRESS

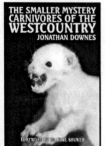

THE SMALLER MYSTERY CARNIVORES OF THE WESTCOUNTRY
Jonathan Downes - ISBN 978-1-905723-05-8

£7.99

Although much has been written in recent years about the mystery big cats which have been reported stalking Westcountry moorlands, little has been written on the subject of the smaller British mystery carnivores. This unique book redresses the balance and examines the current status in the Westcountry of three species thought to be extinct: the Wildcat, the Pine Marten and the Polecat, finding that the truth is far more exciting than the currently held scientific dogma. This book also uncovers evidence suggesting that even more exotic species of small mammal may lurk hitherto unsuspected in the countryside of Devon, Cornwall, Somerset and Dorset.

THE BLACKDOWN MYSTERY
Jonathan Downes - ISBN 978-1-905723-00-3

£7.99

Intrepid members of the CFZ are up to the challenge, and manage to entangle themselves thoroughly in the bizarre trappings of this case. This is the soft underbelly of ufology, rife with unsavoury characters, plenty of drugs and booze." That sums it up quite well, we think. A new edition of the classic 1999 book by legendary fortean author Jonathan Downes. In this remarkable book, Jon weaves a complex tale of conspiracy, anti-conspiracy, quasi-conspiracy and downright lies surrounding an air-crash and alleged UFO incident in Somerset during 1996. However the story is much stranger than that. This excellent and amusing book lifts the lid off much of contemporary forteana and explains far more than it initially promises.

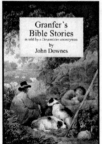

GRANFER'S BIBLE STORIES
John Downes - ISBN 0-9512872-8-1

£7.99

Bible stories in the Devonshire vernacular, each story being told by an old Devon Grandfather - 'Granfer'. These stories are now collected together in a remarkable book presenting selected parts of the Bible as one more-or-less continuous tale in short 'bite sized' stories intended for dipping into or even for bed-time reading. `Granfer` treats the biblical characters as if they were simple country folk living in the next village. Many of the stories are treated with a degree of bucolic humour and kindly irreverence, which not only gives the reader an opportunity to re-evaluate familiar tales in a new light, but do so in both an entertaining and a spiritually uplifting manner.

FRAGRANT HARBOURS DISTANT RIVERS
John Downes - ISBN 0-9512872-5-7

£12.50

Many excellent books have been written about Africa during the second half of the 19th Century, but this one is unique in that it presents the stories of a dozen different people, whose interlinked lives and achievements have as many nuances as any contemporary soap opera. It explains how the events in China and Hong Kong which surrounded the Opium Wars, intimately effected the events in Africa which take up the majority of this book. The author served in the Colonial Service in Nigeria and Hong Kong, during which he found himself following in the footsteps of one of the main characters in this book; Frederick Lugard – the architect of modern Nigeria.

**CFZ PRESS, MYRTLE COTTAGE,
WOOLFARDISWORTHY BIDEFORD,
NORTH DEVON, EX39 5QR
w w w . c f z . o r g . u k**

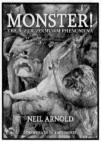

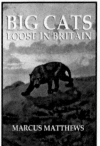

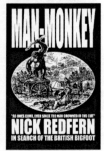

Other books available from
CFZ PRESS

CFZ PRESS

ANIMALS & MEN - Issues 11 - 15 - The Call of the Wild
Jonathan Downes (Ed) - ISBN 978-1-905723-07-2

£12.50

Since 1994 we have been publishing the world's only dedicated cryptozoology magazine, *Animals & Men*. This volume contains fascimile reprints of issues 11 to 15 and includes articles covering out of place walruses, feathered dinosaurs, possible North American ground sloth survival, the theory of initial bipedalism, mystery whales, mitten crabs in Britain, Barbary lions, out of place animals in Germany, mystery pangolins, the barking beast of Bath, Yorkshire ABCs, Molly the singing oyster, singing mice, the dragons of Yorkshire, singing mice, the bigfoot murders, waspman, British beavers, the migo, Nessie, the weird warbling whatsit of the westcountry, the quagga project and much more...

IN THE WAKE OF BERNARD HEUVELMANS
Michael A Woodley - ISBN 978-1-905723-20-1

£9.99

Everyone is familiar with the nautical maps from the middle ages that were liberally festooned with images of exotic and monstrous animals, but the truth of the matter is that the *idea* of the sea monster is probably as old as humankind itself.

For two hundred years, scientists have been producing speculative classifications of sea serpents, attempting to place them within a zoological framework. This book looks at these successive classification models, and using a new formula produces a sea serpent classification for the 21st Century.

CENTRE FOR FORTEAN ZOOLOGY 1999 YEARBOOK
Edited by Jonathan Downes
ISBN 978 -1-905723-24-9

£12.50

The Centre For Fortean Zoology Yearbook is a collection of papers and essays too long and detailed for publication in the CFZ Journal *Animals & Men*. With contributions from both well-known researchers, and relative newcomers to the field, the Yearbook provides a forum where new theories can be expounded, and work on little-known cryptids discussed.

CENTRE FOR FORTEAN ZOOLOGY 1996 YEARBOOK
Edited by Jonathan Downes
ISBN 978 -1-905723-22-5

£12.50

The Centre For Fortean Zoology Yearbook is a collection of papers and essays too long and detailed for publication in the CFZ Journal *Animals & Men*. With contributions from both well-known researchers, and relative newcomers to the field, the Yearbook provides a forum where new theories can be expounded, and work on little-known cryptids discussed.

**CFZ PRESS, MYRTLE COTTAGE,
WOOLFARDISWORTHY BIDEFORD,
NORTH DEVON, EX39 5QR
w w w . c f z . o r g . u k**

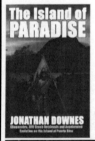

Lightning Source UK Ltd.
Milton Keynes UK
28 October 2010

162032UK00001B/82/P